DIVINE MISSION
Discovering Your Hope and Purpose

Deacon Larry Oney

OSV
INNOVATION

Divine Mission
Written by Larry D. Oney
Copyright © 2017 by Larry D. Oney
Printed in the United States

ISBN: 1979202478
ISBN-13: 978-1979202473

DEDICATION

To Christopher, Adrienne, Jonathan, Michael Jude, and Alex David.
May God give you the grace to discover, enter, and walk
in your divine mission. Love, Dad

CONTENTS

PREFACE

I believe that we are in a strategic time upon the earth in terms of salvation history and we need the Body of Christ to be engaged and to be clear about what our charge is within the mission of Christ. It is not my intent, however to exclude non-believers. I invite all of us to discuss these age-old questions: *"Why am I here? Why was I created?"* The only solution I can offer to these questions points to the Creator. I want to explore during the course of this book the question, *"What is our divine mission upon the earth as someone created by a Sovereign God?"*

Jeremiah 1:5 reads: "Before I formed you in the womb I knew you." So, God, the Creator, knew us even before we were in our mother's womb. It's a mystery but it does speak to this reality: God knew something of us before we were conceived. This Scripture goes on to say, not only did God know us, but, "I dedicated you"—for a purpose! And "I appointed you"—to something specific!

To me this says that God designed you and me with something specific in mind that He wanted us to do upon the earth that is unique to each of us! God has already signaled that He created us for a principal purpose—God just wants us to stop long enough trying to live "a great life," so that we can discover His plan and purpose for the life that He has in mind for us to discover and enter into. He's not trying to hide it from us.

In this book, I will provide some keys on how to discover God's plan and purpose for your life. God is not involved in tricks and deception; He wants us to discover why He's made us in a particular way. Each one of us is different. We are fearfully and wonderfully made:

> I praise you, because I am wonderfully made;
> wonderful are your works!
> My very self you know.
> (Psalm 139:14)

We want to explore how to not only **discover** but **enter into** our divine mission. Once we determine what our mission is, how do we enter the mission which God has created us for, and called us to do, upon this earth? When we talk about "being called" in this book, we are referring to the feeling or sense, a knowing that a Divine Person is calling and directing us toward what He created us to do and be.

Once we discover and enter our divine mission—and entering is a conscious decision—we need to continually walk in our mission. We need to take an affirmative step to enter into it, own it, and claim it so we can look forward; particularly as a member of the Body of Christ. It is important that the members of the Body of Christ be where they're supposed to be. We don't need a nose trying to be a head, a head trying to be a foot, or a foot trying to be an elbow.

> Now the body is not a single part, but many. If a foot should say, "Because I am not a hand I do not belong to the body," it does not for this reason belong any less to the body. Or if an ear should say, "Because I am not an eye I do not belong to the body," it does not for this reason belong any less to the body. If the whole body were an eye, where would the hearing be? If the whole body were hearing, where would the sense of smell be? (1 Corinthians 12:14-17)

In my own life, I began to have a sense of what God was appointing me to. He was appointing me to three specific things: first, to participate in and expand the Kingdom of God, consistent with Matthew 10:7: "As you go, make this proclamation: 'The kingdom of heaven is at hand;'" second, to give people a sense of a hope and a purpose for their lives (Jeremiah 29:11-14); lastly, to help heal the broken-hearted (that is, to attach myself to the materially and spiritually poor). John 10:10 says, "I came so that they might have life and have it more abundantly."

These happen to be the foundational principles of Hope and Purpose Ministries, and that is how it has played out personally for me. Our ministry wants to be involved in expanding the Kingdom of God, helping to heal the broken hearted, and giving people a sense of hope and purpose, which can be found in discovering, entering, and walking in your divine mission!

Discovering Your Divine Mission

CHAPTER 1
DIVINE HOPE

When the Word of God speaks of hope, it never applies to the future only, but also to our present situation. Where we put our hope, our trust, and our security must impact our daily lives. Psalm 130:1b-8 offers three reasons to hope and trust God:

Out of the depths I call to you, LORD;

Lord, hear my cry!

May your ears be attentive

to my cry for mercy.

If you, LORD, keep account of sins,

Lord, who can stand?

But with you is forgiveness

and so you are revered.

I wait for the LORD,

my soul waits

and I hope for his word.

My soul looks for the Lord

more than sentinels for daybreak.

More than sentinels for daybreak,

let Israel hope in the LORD,

For with the LORD is mercy,

with him is plenteous redemption,

And he will redeem Israel

from all its sins.

Throughout the Scriptural history of the nation of Israel, God, through His prophets, always encourages His chosen people to trust in Him. This passage is a prayer and a challenging call for

Israel to trust in God, and a reminder for us that we also should put our hope and trust in God.

The first reason for this trust is the Scripture itself: "I wait for the Lord, my soul waits and I hope for his word." (Psalm 130:5) There is no hint of a lie contained within (see Numbers 23:19). The character of the Lord reflects on the character of the Word, and likewise the character of the Word reflects on the character of the Lord.

Second, the heart of the Lord is full of mercy and kindness. You can be sure that your efforts, your labor, your tears, and your patient waiting will not go to waste, for the object of your hope is merciful. God's mercy is faithful, solid, and strong. Jesus is not moody like us. His mercy and kindness are a steadfast love.

The third reason that we should hope in the Lord is because of God's salvific love for us. He promises to redeem Israel from its sins. In other words, we can wait joyfully for His coming because our hope is based upon His steadfast love.

When I was younger, I grew up in a challenging situation, I remember seeing Christian women working in the fields and they would be singing, "Lord come and rest in me, so that I can rest." That song was based on hope—that God would come and settle in their hearts and keep their hope alive.

What does it mean to hope or to have hope? Pope Francis has taught us what hope is not: "Hope is not optimism; it is not that ability to look at things with good cheer and move on. No, that is optimism; that is not hope. Nor is hope a positive attitude in front of things. Those shiny, positive people . . . it is not hope."[1]

If hope is not seeing the world through rose colored glasses, what is it? In Scripture, the word which translates into the English word "hope" can also be translated as "trust" or "security."

God is the God of redemption (Luke 1:68). He has proven this already by redeeming us from the bondage of sin and death (Galatians 3:13; 4:5), the power of sin that enslaves us (Romans 6:18, 22), the troubles of life (Psalm 25:22), the atmosphere of evil and darkness that influences the world (Psalm 130:8, Titus 2:14, Galatians 1:4), and purposeless conduct that displeases God (1 Peter 1:18). Since the Lord has already proven He is trustworthy and has saved us from our sins, He invites us to put our trust and hope in Him. King David had this type of unshakable hope in God:

I keep the LORD always before me;

with him at my right hand, I shall never be shaken.

Therefore my heart is glad, my soul rejoices;

my body also dwells secure,

For you will not abandon my soul to Sheol,

nor let your devout one see the pit.

You will show me the path to life,

abounding joy in your presence,

the delights at your right hand forever.

(Psalm 16:8-11).

David has a secure hope beyond death. Even his body rests secure. For believers, death is not the end, but rather an entrance to a new beginning—a beginning that is immortal, pure, joyful, and divine. With this view of life, we can face the problems and pains of this life with courage and rest securely because the Lord is at our right hand.

We can experience this kind of hope if we have an awareness of the presence of the Lord and trust that the Lord will be on our side. It does not matter where you have come from, what the color of your skin is, what gender you are, or what you have done in the past. *Your history does not determine your destiny* with God! God looks over our past failings and extends His abundant mercy to us if we are sorry for our sins and ask for forgiveness. No matter what we have been through or what we have done; we were created by God to accomplish our Divine Mission.

Gideon, (Judges 6 to 8), is one example of how God selects a person despite his current or past situation. Gideon did not think much of himself and he acted cowardly. Yet, despite, all of

Gideon's shortcomings in the eyes of the world, God chose him to save Israel from the Midianites.

God is always faithful. We can hope and trust in God even when we have been unfaithful to Him in the past. God is even faithful when we fall; He is always willing to take us back. We can look at the Book of Hosea to see where God's steadfast love is demonstrated.

Our God is a God of truth. The clear and strong reason why our hope of eternal life will be fulfilled is because we have a God who is true to His promises. This is why we can wait in joyful hope. If there is one thing that is impossible for God to do, it is lie. "God is not a human being who speaks falsely, nor a mortal, who feels regret. Is God one to speak and not act, to decree and not bring it to pass?" (Numbers 23:19) And so, the surety of Christian hope is the truthful character of God.

Many people will wonder why I am starting with hope, instead of getting right to telling you what your purpose is. It is not for me to say what your purpose is, rather, I am trying to help you discover your divine purpose and how to enter and walk in it. St. Teresa of Avila gives us some good insight into why we should not skip over hope and go straight to our purpose:

> "Let nothing disturb you
>
> Let nothing frighten you
>
> All things are passing away

God never changes

Patience obtains all things

Whoever has God lacks nothing

God alone suffices."

We are made in the image of God and our purpose is to grow into the likeness of God. This will not happen totally on earth, but we must strive toward it. Like the Incarnation when the Word became flesh, Jesus still had to grow in wisdom and stature. "And Jesus grew in wisdom and stature, and in favor with God and man." (Luke 2:52, NIV)

Ultimately, the difference between Christian hope and other types of hope is that the hope of the Christian is certain and objective because it is rooted in God Himself. St. Paul was in prison when he wrote to the Church at Philippi, "for I know that this will result in deliverance for me through your prayers and support from the Spirit of Jesus Christ. My eager expectation and hope is that I shall not be put to shame in any way, but that with all boldness, now as always, Christ will be magnified in my body, whether by life or death. For to me life is Christ." (Philippians 1:19-21a)

Paul was suffering for the Gospel when he wrote this. His situation was not comfortable. Despite that, his hope allowed him to be bold for Jesus and to dedicate his life only to Him. His was a passionate hope, made possible by prayer and the Spirit of Jesus

Christ. As a direct result, he was unashamed to proclaim Christ, to live for Christ, and ultimately, to die for Christ.

Paul is encouraging believers to never give up in their walk with God, although they may face hardships and troubles in this world because of their relationship with Christ. We can see here again the same principle which the Scriptures repeatedly teach us: Christian hope is not earthly and human. Rather it is divine and eternal.

Part of the challenge, as Pope Benedict XVI acknowledges, is that, "we who have always lived with the Christian concept of God, and have grown accustomed to it, have almost ceased to notice that we possess the hope that ensues from a real **encounter** with this God."[2]

We acknowledge Jesus Christ as our Savior. We believe that he rose from the dead. We may attend Mass and perhaps even engage in prayer occasionally, but it may have become commonplace; simply part of our routine. God asks us to strive to become fully aware, to pay attention to this great gift that we have been given. In the context of the Mass, we are exhorted to be present, physically and emotionally, and to have a full, active participation in the liturgy:

> The celebrating assembly is the community of the baptized who, "by regeneration and the anointing of the Holy Spirit, are consecrated to be a spiritual house and a holy priesthood, that through all the works of Christian men they may offer spiritual

sacrifices." This "common priesthood" is that of Christ the sole priest, in which all his members participate:

> Mother Church earnestly desires that all the faithful should be led to that full, conscious, and active participation in liturgical celebrations which is demanded by the very nature of the liturgy, and to which the Christian people, "a chosen race, a royal priesthood, a holy nation, a redeemed people," have a right and an obligation by reason of their Baptism. (CCC, 1141)

We need to look at this reality with fresh eyes. The early Christians were in awe of the Good News of Jesus. This was a whole new way of approaching life. What does this eternal life offer? Is it something that we should want? St. Paul tells us, "What eye has not seen, and ear has not heard, and what has not entered the human heart, what God has prepared for those who love him," (1 Corinthians 2:9b). He teaches that the world beyond this one is beyond anything we can imagine. The Book of Revelation speaks of a great multitude wearing white robes, "who have survived the time of great distress; they have washed their robes and made them white in the blood of the Lamb. . . They will not hunger or thirst anymore, nor will the sun or any heat strike them. For the Lamb who is in the center of the throne will shepherd them and lead them to springs of life-giving water, and God will wipe away every tear from their eyes." (Revelation 7:14b-17).

How does one answer the questions: where am I going? What was I made to do? What does my eternal future look like? What am I supposed to do with my life? How does one position oneself to enter into the eternal life that we have just described? We Christians should be happy, not because God always does what we want, but because our hope is based on God's will for us. Christian hope is the "hope of the just" (Proverbs 10:28) because we put our hope and trust in a just and faithful God as revealed to us through Scripture, through the Person of Jesus Christ, and the animation of the Holy Spirit.

The only way to enter into a life that is full of hope is by an **encounter** with the Person of Jesus Christ and the power of the Holy Spirit!

Our Divine Hope is found in the

Person of Jesus Christ.

Trust in Jesus.

CHAPTER 2
DIVINE ENCOUNTER

What does it mean to have a **Divine Encounter** with the Person of Jesus Christ? Before we can begin to discover our Divine Purpose, we need to connect with Jesus. He's the one who is going to tell us where we need to go and what we need to be doing in our lives, and if we aren't tuned in we aren't going to get the message. Jesus is the reason for our hope and the Person in whom we place our trust.

No doubt you've seen people holding signs at sporting events proclaiming John 3:16— "For God so loved the world that he gave his only Son, so that everyone who believes in him might not perish but have eternal life." That one verse sums up salvation history!

People in the New Testament were fortunate—they had the opportunity to have a personal **encounter** with the living, breathing Person of Jesus while He walked on the earth. Andrew and John—the sons of Zebedee—had been followers of John the Baptist and were the first to follow the Lord. Andrew was the brother of Simon and brought him to Jesus. As soon as Jesus met Simon, He changed his name to Peter, which means "rock" (see Mark 3:16, Matthew 16:18, and John 1:42). Although this was only his first meeting with the Son of God, Peter was forever changed. That is what can happen to you as well once you open your heart and mind to the Person of Jesus Christ and experience an **encounter** with Him through the pages of this book. This is an opportunity to have a new **encounter** with the Person of Jesus Christ, right now!

Peter would be the one to publicly declare that Jesus was, in fact, the promised Messiah. Jesus asked His disciples who people said that He was. The disciples responded with various answers that some people said he was, including Elijah and John the Baptist. He then asked, "'But who do you say that I am?' Simon Peter said in reply, 'You are the Messiah, the Son of the Living God'" (Matthew 16:15b-16). Immediately after this testimony, Jesus declares, "you are Peter, and upon this rock I will build my church, and the gates of the netherworld shall not prevail against it. I will give you the keys to the kingdom of heaven." (Matthew 16:18b-19a).

Peter was also one of the chosen ones who saw a vision of the glorified Christ at the Transfiguration (Matthew 17) and was assured by Jesus that because he and the other apostles had given up everything to follow Him they would inherit eternal life and would sit on thrones (Matthew 19:28-29).

The declaration that Peter was the one chosen to lead the Church did not mean that he was perfect. Far from it. Peter was human like the rest of us. In fact, we can take great comfort in his humanity, because if Jesus could work with Peter, who was a little rough around the edges, He can certainly work with us!

When Jesus told His apostles that He would have to go to Jerusalem to suffer and die in order to be raised on the third day, Peter failed to understand that this was necessary for God's plan of salvation. Instead, he protested, "God forbid, Lord! No such thing shall ever happen to you." Jesus quickly rebuked him in very harsh terms. "Get behind me, Satan! . . . You are thinking not as God does, but as human beings do." (Matthew 16:22b-23) Peter suffered from the same misguided emotion in the Garden of Gethsemane. When the soldiers came to arrest Jesus, Peter was ready to fight them with his sword, cutting off the high priest slave's ear. "Jesus said to Peter, 'Put your sword into its scabbard. Shall I not drink the cup that the Father gave me?'" (John 18:11).

Later, we read of Peter's ultimate moment of weakness. All four gospels report that as Jesus was held in custody and tried,

Peter denied Him three times. Peter denied that he even *knew* Jesus. We can learn something very important about having a relationship with Jesus from how Peter reacts afterwards. He does not avoid Jesus. He doesn't go into hiding for fear of what Jesus will do or say to him. Instead, Peter returns to his role as a beloved apostle. He is one of the first apostles that Mary Magdalene tells about the empty tomb and Peter rushes to the tomb to see for himself if what she says is true.

Finally, we see Peter's final **encounter** with the Lord which is recorded in Scripture. Echoing Peter's triple denial, the Lord asks Peter three times if he loves Him. Peter answers, "Yes, Lord, you know that I love you," each time. After this, Jesus instructs Peter to take care of His sheep; meaning the Church that He leaves behind (John 21:15-17).

Peter is forgiven. He is blessed by Jesus and given an important job to do. Peter is evidence that Jesus will not abandon us even if we mess up. He is a God of second and third and seventy-times-seven chances. He will forgive us and welcome us back. All we have to do is ask. Peter is an example of the hopeful statement that I love to recall: *our history does not determine our destiny.*

Nicodemus is another man who had a powerful **encounter** with Jesus. Unlike Peter, who was a fisherman and a member of the working class, Nicodemus held a place of power in Jewish society. He was a Pharisee and a member of the Sanhedrin—the Jewish council—who came to Jesus under the cover of night to question and learn from Him. He recognizes that Jesus comes from God.

Jesus instructs him that "no one can enter the kingdom of God without being born of water and Spirit." (John 3:5b) The Lord chastises Nicodemus, who is supposed to be a Jewish teacher, for not understanding, but Nicodemus must have been transformed by the experience because he is later ready to come out of the darkness of night and declare himself publicly as a follower of Jesus—in a potentially deadly move. He defends Jesus' right to be interrogated before being judged in John 7:50-52, and after Jesus' death, he assists Joseph of Arimathea in burying His body. We do not know much about Nicodemus; however, we do know that after meeting Jesus, he was never the same. He was willing to risk his place of power and prestige for the Lord. Like Nicodemus, we can open ourselves to the possibility of being transformed by an **encounter** with Jesus Christ. We can prepare ourselves to never be the same!

We have a choice in whether or not we will respond to the call of an **encounter** with Christ. We always have free will. The rich young man in Matthew 19:16-30, came to Jesus with the best of intentions. He wanted to know what he had to do to gain eternal life. Jesus tells him the starting point: he needs to obey the commandments. Jesus then lists them. This was a good young man; probably better than most of us. After all, he claims that he has obeyed the commandments all his life—*all* of them. How many of us can say that? The young man wants to know more. What more can he do? This is an important point. When we have an **encounter** with Jesus—when we come to Him with a humble heart and ask, *"What more can I do,"* He will provide an answer, so we need to be ready.

How did Jesus respond to the rich young man? He tells the young man, "If you wish to be perfect, go, sell what you have and give to the poor, and you will have treasure in heaven. Then come, follow me." (Matthew 19:21b) This is a tall order and the young man "went away sad, for he had many possessions." (Matthew 19:22b) It is important to state again that this was a devout young man. He truly wanted to do the will of God, but he came across a stumbling block that kept him from following Jesus completely. For him the stumbling block was money. He had plans for his life, but Jesus had a different plan—a better plan. The rich young man wasn't ready to take that next step.

Jesus isn't necessarily asking each of us to give up all our material possessions. This was the request that He made of this particular young man and he was unable to do as he was asked. Jesus might be asking us to give up something else, or begin doing something else, and we might have our own stumbling blocks that prevent us from following Him wholeheartedly. He might be asking us to change careers or to change the focus of our work. He might ask us to overcome our history. We might be telling Jesus that we can't do what He asks because of something that we have done in our past. Jesus might be asking us to stop holding on to our past sins. Can we do that? Can we move forward and trust the Lord? Jesus might be asking us to surrender our plans and our dreams. Like the rich young man, we might have a vision for our life; something that we have worked hard to achieve. Jesus might be saying, "I have a better plan." Can we lay down our plans and dreams and follow Him?

Regardless of what Jesus is asking us in particular to do, He always wants us to put God first: before our spouse, our children, our parents, our job, and even our very lives. All those things are important; however, God needs to come first. God will then help us to put all the other people and things in our lives in their proper place of importance. We can trust Jesus. He has the best plan for our lives.

With the exception of perhaps Mary, the Mother of God, who certainly had the most profound relationship with Jesus, Mary Magdalene is one of the women in Scripture who was most dramatically changed by her **encounter** with Christ. She is identified in Luke 8:2 as a woman, "from whom seven demons had gone out." She was healed by Jesus—body and soul. Her illnesses were cured; her sins were forgiven. What a dramatic transformation of her life! She **encountered** Jesus and was healed. Her life was never the same and she became His follower without ever looking back.

Mary Magdalene would stand by Jesus at His moment of suffering; while with the exception of John, His apostles were nowhere to be found. Mary Magdalene and several other women were there to support Him in His time of need.

Jesus had plans for Mary Magdalene as well. All four Gospels testify to the fact that Mary Magdalene was one of the first witnesses to the Resurrection. She is known as the "Apostle to the Apostles" because she was the one to tell them that the Lord had risen. This woman who had suffered so much would become a great Saint.

Paul is another person who had a dramatic conversion as a result of an **encounter** with Christ. In his case, it was an **encounter** with the glorified Christ who had already ascended into heaven. He did not know Jesus while the Lord walked on the earth. Before Jesus renamed Paul, his name was Saul. As Saul, he was a zealous Jew and was determined to root out the so-called followers of "the Way," who were preaching and following the tenets Jesus. He was present at the martyrdom of Stephen, a deacon, (Acts 7:58), and "was trying to destroy the church; entering house after house and dragging out men and women, he handed them over for imprisonment." (Acts 8:3b). He thought he was doing what God wanted him to do.

With the permission of the high priest, Saul headed toward Damascus on a mission to round up even more of these new Christians—followers of the Way.

> On his journey, as he was nearing Damascus, a light from the sky suddenly flashed around him. He fell to the ground and heard a voice saying to him, "Saul, Saul, why are you persecuting me?" He said, "Who are you, sir?" The reply came, "I am Jesus, whom you are persecuting. Now get up and go into the city and you will be told what you must do." (Acts 9:3-6).

When the vision faded, Saul was blind. Jesus then spoke to Ananias and sent him to Saul to lay his hands on him and heal him. Ananias wasn't overly excited about this assignment. Sometimes God gives us a Divine Assignment that might not be initially appealing to us. He still asks us to act in faith and not in what appears to be. (More on Divine Assignment in a later chapter.)

He had heard about Saul and knew how he felt about the followers of Christ; however, he found Saul to be a changed man. Once the scales fell from his eyes Saul was baptized and began to preach to the people about Jesus. Nobody knew what to make of him and the Jews conspired to kill him, but the disciples of the Lord helped him escape. He chose to go by his Greek name—

Paul—and spent the rest of his life preaching about Jesus to the Gentiles. Paul was ultimately martyred for the faith in Rome.

Paul was always filled with passion and zeal. God took the gifts He had bestowed upon Paul and turned him towards using these gifts for His divine purposes. Paul needed something dramatic to get his attention, and God in the person of the glorified Christ provided it, utterly transforming Paul by the **encounter**; his life would never be the same.

In looking at these individuals—Peter, Nicodemus, Mary Magdalene, and Paul—we have explored four people whose lives were completely changed by **encountering** the Person of Jesus. They discovered their hope and purpose in their relationship with Him.

You may be saying at this point, "Yes, but these people were all Saints, and their experiences are not exactly relevant to my own life." After all, we don't live two thousand years ago when Jesus walked the earth. He isn't going to call us to follow Him when we are out fishing or show up at the local hospital to heal us of our physical and mental illnesses. No bright light is going to come out of nowhere as we are driving home from work. What does all this have to do with us? But these examples of these **encounters** point to an opportunity for a metanoia, (a change in direction of life). All lives are different, but these examples show that Jesus can come into any life situation.

It is good here to ask, what do you long for in life? We all long for something. No matter how many people we have in our lives who love us, no matter how much money we have in the bank, or how famous we might be, we all have a hole in our hearts that we spend our lives trying to fill. People can try to fill that void with lots of things. Some people try to work the hole away. If they can just get that next job promotion, maybe the longing will go away. Other people turn to money. If they can get a certain amount of money in their bank account, everything will be perfect. Still others turn to food, or drugs, or alcohol, or sex. Here's the secret, though: no matter how much we seek of these things, that void will still be there. Even the love of another person, as good and important as that is, can't completely fill the void. St. Augustine said it best: "Our hearts are restless until they rest in You." The "you" in St. Augustine's quote is God. Only God can fill that emptiness, that sense of a void, that sense of longing.

How then can we have a **Divine Encounter** with the Person of Jesus? How can we invite the Lord Jesus to touch our lives and transform us? The answer is simple: all we have to do is ask!

If you have not had an **encounter** with the Lord Jesus, I propose the following. I invite you right now to just stand if you can and open your arms wide and say simply, "Lord Jesus, I give you permission to come into my heart and make Yourself known to me." Then say, "Come Holy Spirit! Come and fill me with your presence." If you prayed this simple prayer with a sincere heart, you have now opened yourself to an **encounter** with the Person of Jesus Christ. And when you prayed, "Come Holy Spirit," you have invited the Prime Animator of the designs of God upon the earth to lead and direct your life to accomplish the plan and purpose in your life that God planned for you before you were formed in your mother's womb. (Jer. 1:5) Some people would describe this as you have now been *baptized in the Holy Spirit* through this prayer. Which now means that you have the possibility of exercising all of the gifts of the Holy Spirit as mentioned in First Corinthians chapters 12 and 14. I strongly recommend that you pause and read both of those chapters in your personal Bible right now.

For those who have already received the Sacrament of Baptism, this is not a new water baptism, but a *baptism of the Holy Spirit*; whom you received at both the Sacraments of Baptism and Confirmation. This prayer invites the Holy Spirit, whom you received during the sacraments, to move and act in and through you, if you prayed with a sincere heart.

Perhaps you have seen that famous picture of Jesus knocking on the door to a house waiting to be let inside. That house is our hearts. Jesus is knocking on the door wanting to enter our hearts. All we have to do is open ourselves up to Him. He wants us just as we are right now. Are you in a state of sin? Open your heart to

Jesus and ask for His merciful heart to forgive you and give you a new beginning. Are you suffering from physical, emotional, or mental illness? Open your heart to Jesus. Do you consider yourself spiritual but not religious? Open your heart to Jesus. Do you try to lead a good life but don't feel like you have ever had a personal **encounter** with the Lord? Today is that day! Open your heart to Jesus!

You don't need any fancy words. The prayers "Come, Lord Jesus" and "Come, Holy Spirit" are powerful. Jesus is waiting. The Spirit is waiting. All we have to do is say "yes" to their invitation. He will not refuse your request for Him to enter your heart. He, "is able to accomplish far more than all we ask or imagine." (Ephesians 3:20b) Will you say yes and allow Jesus to transform your life? Your answer makes all the difference.

A Divine Encounter with the Person of Jesus Christ happens when you say, "yes" to the invitation He is always offering to you.

CHAPTER 3
DIVINE PREPARATION

Now that you have invited the Son of God and the Holy Spirit into your life more fully through prayer, you are ready to begin your "Divine Preparation" for your Divine Mission as a son or daughter of God. Divine Preparation has many components. There is preparation before we host God, before beginning our mission, and before each assignment. Sometimes we may not even notice that we are being prepared until afterwards when we look back and see it as a time of preparation. There are many ways to prepare. We will explore a few of those ways in this section; however, this will not be an exhaustive list. Some ways to generally prepare are: prayer, praise, participating in the Sacraments, fasting (if called), reading the Bible, studying the Word of God, fellowship with other Christians, and learning to serve in a humble and obedient manner.

We do have to prepare to host the presence of God. One of the ways in which we do this is to admit that we are all sinners, and that we are in need of God's grace and His mercy. Making a good Confession is a good way to begin to prepare a clean vessel to host the presence of God! If we want to enter into our divine mission and assignments, we need to begin with beginning again—that is, beginning in the mercy that is poured out by God.

We also need to recognize that Divine Preparation can sometimes take a long time or can happen in an unexpected way. Jesus spent 30 years preparing for a mission that lasted less than 3 years. David was a shepherd boy who was preparing to be the king of Israel—he was tending sheep. Then suddenly the prophet of God appeared in his life and called him to his Divine Mission. We might have a task or job right now that feels like tending sheep, and we might be out of sight for most people; however, it is a time of preparation for us that can be very valuable.

You might be doing a job in which no one can see you right now, or that seems unimportant. Know that you might be in the middle of your divine preparation for entering into your divine mission that God has called you to. We should try to do everything that God has allowed us to do, and do it to the best of our ability.

There is a component to Divine Preparation that we are to participate in fully. We must prepare ourselves to host God by dealing with our past issues and sins and by doing our part to become a holy dwelling place for the Lord. Using discernment in all things will help us to choose those actions and activities that will draw us closer to God.

A second component of Divine Preparation that we should always be open to is the preparation that God does for each of us. God prepares us to be able to say "yes" to Him in different ways. This preparation is unique to each of us because God sees each of us individually. God loves you! God knows you—the deepest parts of you. He recognizes that you may have a need that someone else may not have, or vice versa.

> LORD, you have probed me, you know me: you know when I sit and stand; you understand my thoughts from afar. You sift through my travels and my rest; with all my ways you are familiar. (Psalm 139:1b-3)

Here are some other ways that God prepares all of us—He prepares our heart with His grace and our being with His mercy. God's grace flows to each person; whether they know about it at the time, acknowledge it, or doubt it. God's mercy can be seen through His Son, Jesus, and in His death on Calvary and His Resurrection. God's mercy can be seen through the gift of the Holy Spirit at Pentecost and in many instances since then.

It is by the guidance of the Holy Spirit that you are reading this book; whether you purchased it, or it was a gift from someone else. God prepares us to hear what we need to hear and to see what we need to see to be ready to say "yes" to Him. The Sacraments of Baptism and Confirmation are both ways that God helps to prepare us.

One final way that God prepares everyone that must not be overlooked is God's love. God loves you! This cannot be overstated. Some people have never heard that God loves him or her. Or if they have heard it, they do not always believe it. The truth is that God really does love you and me and everyone else on the earth. God's love is not like human love that can sometimes be conditional or suffer from the influence of human emotions of inconstancy.

> But the wisdom from above is first of all pure, then peaceable, gentle, compliant, full of mercy and good fruits, without inconstancy or insincerity. (James 3:17)

God's love is pure and does not waver in its strength. God's love was so powerful that He gave His only Son, Jesus Christ. So great was the love of Jesus that He went to the Cross for our sins and transgressions. Out of the love of The Father and the Son, the Holy Spirit is given as a lasting sign of that love—to guide us through this world and into eternal life with The Father.

As we will discuss more in later chapters, our Divine Mission and each Divine Assignment that we are given also comes with preparation. We must be prepared for the Mission and

Assignments that we are given, and that preparation is offered by the power of the Holy Spirit.

When God gives us a Divine Assignment, He will also give us an anointing for that Assignment. Baptized Christians are given baptism, just like Jesus. Before he began His divine mission upon the earth, Jesus went down to the Jordan River to be baptized by John, as part of His preparation, because He was both fully man and fully God. When He came out of the waters of the Jordan River, the Holy Spirit descended upon Him. Today, Christians are baptized in the name of The Father, and The Son, and The Holy Spirit. We become part of the Divine Family through Baptism and Confirmation. We receive the Holy Spirit at Baptism and Confirmation. It is this divinity with us, through the Holy Spirit, that we are able to discover, enter, and walk in our Divine Mission upon the Earth.

Some general ways to prepare ourselves for our Divine Mission are to pray and to praise God. Prayer is one of the most important aspects of the Christian lifestyle. Prayer can take many forms. The Church teaches us that there are different types of prayer: blessing and adoration, prayer of petition, prayer of intercession, prayer of thanksgiving, and prayer of praise. Praise is a key component of preparing ourselves for our mission. The benefits and power of praise are manifold:

- Praise changes the atmosphere. (That is, when we praise, it changes the spiritual dynamics of where we are.)
- Praise opens up the manifold blessings of God
- Praise acts as a weapon when we are in a spiritual battle
- Praise tears down the strongholds in our lives
- Praise brings forth a spirit of humility
- Praise makes us more sensitive to what the Lord is saying to us
- Praise creates an opportunity for a break-through
- Praise brings us into the realm of God's glory
- Praise softens our hearts to the multiple outpourings of the Holy Spirit
- Praise scatters the enemies of God
- Praise defeats the designs of the enemy
- Praise releases the fragrance of Heaven
- Praise helps us to host the presence of God

It is the Holy Spirit who teaches believers to pray.

> In the same way, the Spirit too comes to the aid of our weakness; for we do not know how to pray as we ought, but the Spirit itself intercedes with inexpressible groanings. (Romans 8:26)

Why is it important to pray? We need to stay close to God and one of the best ways to know the heart of God is through prayer. As we begin our prayer life, we may only be familiar with the prayer of petition—asking God for what we need or want. Yet, as we grow in our prayer life, we will begin to use other forms of prayer until our prayer of praise is the most often used. This does not mean that we will not put our petitions before God anymore; rather it means that we will more readily praise God because we know of His generosity toward us.

We should also read the Scripture regularly as part of our continuing preparation. Reading the Scripture is not the same as studying Scripture. Reading Scripture helps us to begin to know God and His salvific plan for us and of His great love for us. When we read the Scriptures, it can be a casual reading—like we would with any book. We can take in information, we can be entertained, and we may even get "lost in the pages" and read for longer than intended. Studying the Word of God; however, means that we sit down to examine what the Scriptures are teaching us about the heart and mind of God as He interacts with His people. Praying the Scripture is also another component that is key. *Lectio Divina* (Latin for "Divine Reading," it is the face upon the Word of God) is a method for praying with the Scriptures.

SEVEN (7) KEYS TO REMEMBER
ABOUT DIVINE PREPARATION

God prepares a person for his/her Divine Mission.

But as it is written: "What eye has not seen, and ear has not heard, and what has not entered the human heart, what God has prepared for those who love him," this God has revealed to us through the Spirit. (1 Corinthians 2:9-10a)

Sanctification often comes before manifestation and occupation.

Joshua also said to the people, "Sanctify yourselves, for tomorrow the LORD will perform wonders among you." (Joshua 3:5)

"That is what some of you used to be; but now you have had yourselves washed, you were sanctified, you were justified in the name of the Lord Jesus Christ and in the Spirit of our God." (1 Corinthians 6:11)

Our meditation and contemplation should lead to a proclamation and a demonstration of the power of God.

[A]nd my message and my proclamation were not with persuasive (words of) wisdom, but with a demonstration of spirit and power, so that your faith might rest not on human wisdom but on the power of God. (1 Corinthians 2:4-5)

We were created for our Divine Mission.

For we are his handiwork, created in Christ Jesus for the good works that God has prepared in advance, that we should live in them. (Ephesians 2:10)

✦—✳ We are to assist God with our preparation.

Prepare and get ready, you and the company mobilized for you, but in my service. (Ezekiel 38:7)

...and your feet shod in readiness for the gospel of peace. (Ephesians 6:15)

"Go through the camp and tell the people, 'Get your provisions ready. Three days from now you will cross the Jordan here to go in and take possession of the land the Lord your God is giving you for your own.'" (Joshua 1:11)

✦—✳ As part of our Divine Preparation, God equips us for what we need.

The horse is equipped for the day of battle, but victory is the LORD's. (Proverbs 21:31)

When they hand you over, do not worry about how you are to speak or what you are to say. You will be given at that moment what you are to say. (Matthew 10:19)

✦—✳ Prayer and Thanksgiving are two important components of Divine Preparation.

Persevere in prayer, being watchful in it with thanksgiving. (Colossians 4:2)

In all circumstances give thanks, for this is the will of God for you in Christ Jesus. (1 Thessalonians 5:18)

One example of the difference between reading and studying the Word of God can be illustrated using the story of the woman who anointed the feet of Jesus in Luke 7:36-50. I can read about the woman who bathed the feet of Jesus with her tears and her hair and then anointed His feet with ointment. I can enjoy the story and learn what happened. I might think about the story later or I might not. If I were studying the Scriptures however, I would learn that this was expensive ointment that she used on the feet of Jesus. I would learn that this "sinful woman" was a woman with a history and may have been a prostitute. Through study, I could discover the importance of anointing one's head, washing the feet of a guest (or at least providing water for them to do so), and various other elements about a foreign culture. These may seem like small details; however, by learning them, the Scripture takes on a new richness that illustrates the love of Christ to us even more profoundly. These are not simple details; rather they are the truths about our lives and about how Jesus came to save us. We study the Word of God to show ourselves approved, not unto men, but unto God.

> Be eager to present yourself as acceptable to God, a workman who causes no disgrace, imparting the word of truth without deviation. (2 Timothy 2:15)

We should also try to enjoy fellowship with other Christians, participate in opportunities for growing in the Spirit, and to learn to serve others. Timothy served Paul; Joshua served Moses; the disciples served Jesus while He was preparing them to receive their assignments. A sign of someone ready to take the next step in their spiritual growth and their assignment is when they are open to be led by others who have more experience or are more spiritually mature.

Divine Preparation is both a preparation done by you and by God for you.

Divine Preparation happens before your Divine Mission is given and before each Divine Assignment. It is a continual process by you and by God to help you succeed in all of your Divine callings as we offer ourselves up to participate in the priestly, prophetic, and kingly mission of Jesus.

Entering Your Divine Mission

DEACON LARRY ONEY

44

CHAPTER 4
DIVINE PURPOSE

[T]hen the LORD God formed the man out of the dust of the ground and blew into his nostrils the breath of life, and the man became a living being. (Genesis 2:7)

You formed my inmost being; you knit me in my mother's womb. I praise you, because I am wonderfully made; wonderful are your works! My very self you know. My bones are not hidden from you, When I was being made in secret, fashioned in the depths of the earth. (Psalm 139:13-15)

These two Scripture passages point to the fact that God made us; each one of us individually and for a distinct purpose. Our Divine Purpose is the reason for our existence. When God made us, and gave us His breath (*Ruah Kadesh*), it came with a purpose. God values each person for his or her uniqueness that came from the mind of God. Each person is special and uniquely qualified for his or her Divine Purpose. For the sake of clarity, Divine Purpose is being defined here as your unique calling based on your individual being; which is comprised of your personality, your gifts and talents, and your unique individual circumstances. God knew the situation that you would be in—your social, economic, and belief system. All of these influences help to shape how you view yourself and the world around you. All of these factors (personality, gifts, talents, and influencers), help to make up who you are.

In all of creation, there has never been another you with your particular mix of talents and gifts. We are each a unique and wonderful creation. This is an amazing gift, but it also carries with it a great responsibility. God has a purpose in mind for us; a job only we can do in our own unique way, a distinct calling if you will.

Jeremiah was a prophet who had a Divine Purpose—to be a prophet for God. The people of Israel were in slavery and they cried out to God. They felt that God had forgotten them, but God hadn't forgotten. He decided that he was going to raise up and appoint Jeremiah to speak for Him to the Hebrew people, who were in slavery at the time. The Lord spoke to Jeremiah:

Before I formed you in the womb I knew you,

before you were born I dedicated you,

a prophet to the nations I appointed you.

"Ah, Lord GOD!" I said,

"I do not know how to speak. I am too young!"

But the LORD answered me,

Do not say, "I am too young."

To whomever I send you, you shall go;

whatever I command you, you shall speak.

(Jeremiah 1:5-7)

Just as some of us are afraid to accept our Divine Purpose, (our Divine Calling), Jeremiah was afraid too. He gave God what he no doubt felt were very good excuses: "I do not know how to speak. I am too young." We give God excuses sometimes as well. *I'm too young. I'm too old. I do not have enough financial resources. I'm too broken. I do not have the confidence. I am afraid of failure.*

But God spoke to Jeremiah and He speaks to us as well. "Before you were in your mother's womb, I knew you." Think about that for a minute. This is amazing! God knew you and I even before we were conceived. God appointed Jeremiah as a prophet to the nations before he was even born. God also has plans for each one of us. God made you and I in a particular way; for a particular time; for a particular moment. God has made you and I to exist for such a time as this. We could have been created for any other time, but God chose us to be here at this precise moment by divine design. When God asks us to do something, we can rest assured that we have the skills and gifts necessary to do it. We don't have to be afraid of what God is asking us to do. We can trust God.

Gideon was another reluctant prophet who hesitated in responding to his divine mission. In a lot of ways Gideon is like us. The Israelites were under the power of Midian for seven years and were suffering a great deal. It was a time of misery. An angel of the Lord appeared to Gideon and addressed him: "The LORD is with you, you mighty warrior!" (Judges 6:12b). Listen to that salutation: "you mighty warrior!" Gideon certainly didn't feel like a mighty warrior. He felt like anything but a champion. He felt insignificant and apparently had a poor self-image.

But the Lord replies, I haven't abandoned your people. I'm sending *you*! *You* are going to save Israel. You can almost see Gideon looking around, saying, "You can't possibly be talking to me. You must have someone else in mind."

God's vision for Gideon was bigger than Gideon's vision for himself. He sees himself as small and insignificant, but God made him especially for this great purpose. God knew the important role that Gideon would play in the history of the Israelites since before Gideon was born. Even if we have been weak and afraid in the past and have faced many problems, God can still call you and me and use us for His work. He had it in mind before we were even born!

Jeremiah and Gideon are examples of two people who did not feel "special." They did not see their value or understand their Divine Purpose. There is a wonderful saying that is very true: God doesn't call the qualified; He qualifies the called. God will give you the tools you need to do the assignment He has for you. Just like Jeremiah and Gideon, God has bigger plans for you than the plans you may have for yourself. He knows what you are capable of; because He made you! He can see the whole picture of your life. It doesn't matter what you have done up to this point. *Your history does not determine your destiny*! Today is a new day because you have given yourself to the Lord.

Many people are discouraged to even begin to discover their purpose in life because they have the burden of their past, their environment, their family dynamic, etc... When we even look at the Son of Man, Jesus Christ, we see that His family dynamic, His environment, did not deter Him from His Divine Purpose. Jesus had a difficult family situation, with His mother scorned, and probably being gossiped about when she became pregnant without being wed. Jesus' family were immigrants for a few years. They had to leave His homeland for His safety. Despite all of these things, which many of us face, Jesus still kept focused on the Divine Purpose for His life. I want to encourage you to continue to pursue what your Divine Purpose is even while acknowledging past family difficulties, unstable family dynamics, unfairness, or other significant trials in life that you have experienced. Despite all of that, God still calls you. He still wants you to enter into the Divine Purpose for which He created you with all of the past pain, past issues, or past situations. Because the Father, Son, and Holy Spirit have the ability, despite those past things, to shine a light in us and through us, so that we can perceive and grasp what our Divine Purpose is.

In this discussion of Divine Purpose, it is important to discuss the dignity of each person. The world views people by certain criteria—how beautiful they are, how much money they have, what pedigree can they claim, etc... God views people in a different way. He looks into a person's heart. Each person does have dignity and should be respected as a person.

> But the LORD said to Samuel: Do not judge from his appearance or from his lofty stature, because I have rejected him. God does not see as a mortal, who sees the appearance. The LORD looks into the heart. (1 Samuel 16:7)

Jesus looked into Peter's heart and knew that he would become a mighty apostle. Jesus looked at Mary Magdalen and knew that once healed, she would be a devout follower who would serve Him faithfully. Throughout history, God has seen the truth of people, even if they could not see that truth for themselves.

If you are reading this book and feel like you are too young, too old, the "wrong" color or gender, too poor, too uneducated, or too marginalized in whatever way, God is saying to you now, "You are special to me. I made you for a purpose."

**Your Divine Purpose is specific to you because
you are unique and specially made and gifted by God.
Your Divine Purpose is who you are called to be.**

CHAPTER 5
DIVINE MISSION

For I know well the plans I have in mind for you—
oracle of the Lord—plans for your welfare and not
for woe, so as to give you a future of hope. When
you call me, and come and pray to me, I will listen
to you. When you look for me, you will find me.
Yes, when you seek me with all your heart, I will let
you find me—oracle of the Lord—and I will change
your lot. (Jeremiah 29:11-14a)

God has a plan for you, as He has had for every person who has ever lived or will live. In the last chapter, we learned about our Divine Purpose—something that each person is called to be. Our Divine Mission flows from that Divine Purpose. Our Divine Mission is the overall action that we are given to do while on this earth.

Jesus had a Divine Mission for His time upon the earth—the ultimate Divine Mission stated in John 10:10b: "I came so that they might have life and have it more abundantly." Jesus was born to die upon The Cross and to rise three days later—to participate in God's plan for our salvation.

Our mission is intimately connected with the mission of Jesus. In fact, every Christian's mission is part of the mission of Jesus. In his book *Evangelical Catholicism*, George Weigel states that, "The Church does not *have* a mission, as if 'mission' were one among a dozen things the Church does. The Church *is* a mission, and everything the Church does is ordered to that mission, which is the proclamation of the Gospel for the conversion of the world to Christ."

This mission started with the very first apostles when the Church was in its infancy. Jesus had them gather at the Mount of Olives and gave them their final instruction: "Go, therefore, and make disciples of all nations, baptizing them in the name of the Father, and of the Son, and of the Holy Spirit, teaching them to observe all that I have commanded you." (Matthew 28:19-20a) Jesus then ascended into Heaven.

After the Ascension, the apostles of Jesus, together with Mary and some other women, spent nine days in prayer gathered in an upper room. Jesus had told them to wait for the promise of the Father, the gift of the coming of the Holy Spirit. He told them that they would, "be baptized with the holy Spirit" (Acts 1:5b). As they waited, "suddenly there came from the sky a noise like a strong driving wind, and it filled the entire house in which they were. Then there appeared to them tongues as of fire, which parted and came to rest on each one of them. And they were all filled with the holy Spirit and began to speak in different tongues, as the Spirit enabled them to proclaim" (Acts 2:2b-4).

With the power of the Holy Spirit upon them they then went out and began to preach about the Lord to all who would listen, baptizing three thousand persons that very day (see Acts 2:41). Those of us who are alive today are part of that mission of salvation. We are called to go out and spread the faith. We are called to bring Jesus to the world; to share the Good News. Each one of us who is a part of the Body of Christ needs to work to expand the Kingdom of God. That is our very reason for being.

Both Vatican II and Pope St. John Paul II emphasized that all who have been baptized have a part in the priestly, kingly, and prophetic (teaching) mission of Jesus Christ. In his Apostolic Exhortation *Christifideles Laici*, Pope St. John Paul II taught:

The lay faithful are sharers in the priestly mission, for which Jesus offered himself on the cross and continues to be offered in the celebration of the Eucharist for the glory of God and the salvation of humanity. . . "For their work, prayers and apostolic endeavours, their ordinary married and family life, their daily labour, their mental and physical relaxation, if carried out in the Spirit, and even the hardships of life if patiently borne-all of these become spiritual sacrifices acceptable to God through Jesus Christ (cf. 1 Pt 2:5). . .

Through their participation in the prophetic mission of Christ, "who proclaimed the kingdom of his Father by the testimony of his life and by the power of his word"(24), the lay faithful are given the ability and responsibility to accept the gospel in faith and to proclaim it in word and deed, without hesitating to courageously identify and denounce evil. . . .They are also called to allow the newness and the power of the gospel to shine out everyday in their family and social life, as well as to express patiently and courageously in the contradictions of the present age their hope of future glory even "through the framework of their secular life".

Because the lay faithful belong to Christ, Lord and King of the Universe, they share in his kingly mission and are called by him to spread that Kingdom in history. They exercise their kingship as Christians, above all in the spiritual combat in which they seek to overcome in themselves the kingdom of sin (cf. Rom 6:12), and then to make a gift of themselves so as to serve, in justice and in charity, Jesus who is himself present in all his brothers and sisters, above all in the very least (cf. Mt 25:40).

Every time we celebrate the Eucharist, or gather in prayer, or do a work of mercy, we are sharing the Good News. St. Francis encouraged all of the members of his religious community to preach by their deeds. As a result, a famous quote has been attributed to him, "Preach always. When necessary use words." While St. Francis most likely did not speak this phrase word for word, it certainly reflects the spirit of his life and teaching, and has much to offer us today. Sometimes the greatest means of our evangelization is the way in which we lead our lives. In the Gospel of John, Jesus tells us that, "This is how all will know that you are my disciples, if you have love for one another." (John 13:35)

We may not realize it but others are watching us. They know we are professed Christians. Do they see us loving our neighbors? Do they see us joyfully going to church or hear us talking about going to church on a regular basis? Do they feel that we are people of integrity in the workplace? Do we have a reputation of being generous with our personal resources of time, talent, and treasure? Would they agree that we live the Gospel message in an authentic way? We speak loudly with our actions and our witness of life, but this must be in addition to **giving testimony** for the reason for the hope that we have within us; the Person of Jesus Christ.

My own conversion was a direct result of evangelization. My wife was Catholic and called a Catholic deacon that she knew to come and speak with me. He came over and patiently explained the Catholic faith, answering my many questions. As a result of his evangelization, I began my journey into the Catholic faith at the age of 27 years old, without any prior commitment to any church. We need to be like that deacon and always be ready to share our faith with anyone who is willing to listen. (For more on my personal faith journey, please read *Amazed by God's Grace*.)

As Christians, we are always on duty as ambassadors for Jesus Christ. We are to bring God's love, grace, and mercy to the world, wherever we are. It is not an easy task. We are on the job 24/7 but it is the greatest job that we can have, and it offers the greatest reward—better than the biggest paycheck or the best corner office we could ever get from an earthly job. We have the promise of eternal life, the ultimate "abundant life" that Jesus has promised.

While we are all called to participate in the Divine Mission of Jesus, our specific Divine Mission is the action that we are individually called to do that flows from our Divine Purpose. We need to be alert to what God is calling us to do, pray into our Divine Mission, and make the conscious decision to move into our Divine Mission. It is all about following the prompting of the Holy Spirit in our lives and asking God to reveal to us where He wants us to be and what He wants us to do for the Kingdom of God.

We have looked at individuals in the Scripture doing God's work and fulfilling their Divine Missions. But how can we make it personal to our lives? How do we determine what our Divine Mission is at this moment in our lives?

We may feel like some who say, "I don't know what I am doing or where I am going with my life. I just don't have a sense of what I am supposed to be doing." These could be signs that you are outside of your Divine Mission and need to make a change in direction. How do we figure out how to do this?

Before anything else, we pray. We ask, "Lord, what do you want me to do?" and even more directly, "Lord, show me my divine mission, please." Sometimes God will make what we are supposed to be doing very clear. Other times He makes us work a little harder to discover His plan for us. Rest assured, that if we seek to know His plan and purpose for us and we ask with an open and sincere heart, He will reveal it to us. If we are at a point where the path is unclear, here are a couple of keys to help with the process.

First, what do you love? Think about that for just a moment. What do you love to do? In my own life, I love to build people up; which is what I work to do in my ministry and in my every-day life. Sometimes a Divine Mission will come easily and sometimes it won't. Think of Jonah (we will discuss this more in the next chapter). He did not think his Divine Mission was easy. That's why he was trying to run from it. Sometimes we want to run also; however, we need to pay attention to what God is calling us to do.

When we talk about being called, we mean the sense that the Lord is directing us into a new endeavor. It doesn't necessarily mean it will be overnight. Sometimes we need to do further study, make a physical move, or do some training; but we should start taking steps to move into that direction. We have to put in the time and commitment, but God will provide the strength and resources we need to accomplish His goals for us.

SEVEN (7) KEYS TO REMEMBER ABOUT YOUR DIVINE MISSION

⚷→ You must have a fidelity to the mission

For that person must not suppose that he will receive anything from the Lord, since he is a man of two minds, unstable in all his ways. (James 1:7-8)

Key Notes:
God will not give anything to a doubleminded person. What the Scripture is saying here is that we need to be singular in our mission. As Jesus headed toward Jerusalem with an iron will, He would not let anything take Him off of His path off of His Divine Purpose. His city of destiny was Jerusalem. Not even His good friend Peter could stop Him from going there. Jesus had a solid fidelity to His Divine Mission. To enter into your Divine Mission, you will need similar resolve.

We cannot be wishy-washy. For example, even when we are on vacation or enjoying leisure time, we must not forget that we have a Divine Mission. So, our posture and lifestyle must reflect this reality.

⚷→ You must have clarity of the mission

A thief comes only to steal and slaughter and destroy; I came so that they might have life and have it more abundantly. (John 10:10)

All scripture is inspired by God and is useful for teaching, for refutation, for correction, and for training in righteousness, so that one who belongs to God may be competent, equipped for every good work. (2 Timothy 3:16-17)

Key Notes:
You must be familiar with the details of the Divine Mission of Jesus and the Church; as well as your own.

St Jerome said that ignorance of Scripture is ignorance of Christ.

Clarity of the mission calls for us to know what the mission agenda is. That means that we have to have a good working knowledge of the Word of God, the Holy Scripture. It is not necessary to become a Scripture scholar; however, we do need to be familiar with the basic Gospel message of Christ's birth, death, burial, resurrection, and His Second Coming in Glory. Every Christian person should have the reality of the Kerygma firmly in their minds and to be ready to share this basic message at any moment. For St. Paul says that we should be ready to give the reason for the hope in Christ. (See 1 Peter 3:15.)

⚷─⚹ The mission is for the glory of God—not for ourselves

St Paul said, "For I will not dare to speak of anything except what Christ has accomplished through me." (Romans 15:18a)

Key Notes:
Whatever we accomplish, it is for the glory of God, not for ourselves. Recall the sons of Zebedee, James and John, who wanted to sit at the right and left hand of Jesus. They had lost sight of the reality that the work that we do for the Kingdom of God is for the glory of God and not for ourselves.

✥━➤ You will need the power of the Holy Spirit to accomplish your mission!

...by the power of signs and wonders, by the power of the Spirit [of God], so that from Jerusalem all the way around to Illyricum I have finished preaching the gospel of Christ. (Romans 15:19)

"Not by might, and not by power, but by my spirit, says the Lord of hosts." (Zechariah 4:6b)

Key Notes:
In Acts, Chapter 1, before Jesus ascended into Heaven, He told the disciples to wait for the promise of the Father. The promise of the Father is the Holy Spirit. Jesus was telling the disciples that they were not going to be able to accomplish their mission without the power of the Holy Spirit. In the Mass, we say that we believe in the Holy Spirit, the Lord, the Giver of Life. Not only must we believe in the Holy Spirit, we must continually open ourselves us to the action and prompting and fresh anointing of the Holy Spirit in our lives.

✥━➤ You will need prayer support

In the same way, the Spirit too comes to the aid of our weakness; for we do not know how to pray as we ought, but the Spirit itself intercedes with inexpressible groanings. (Romans 8:26)

Key Notes:
Intercessors and intercession are necessary for success. St. Paul often speaks of his prayer for the community and his intercession for them. For example, in Colossians 1:1-8:

"Paul, an apostle of Christ Jesus by the will of God, and Timothy our brother, to the holy ones and faithful brothers in Christ in Colossae: grace to you and peace from God our Father. We always give thanks to God, the Father of our Lord Jesus Christ, when we pray for you, for we have heard of your faith in Christ Jesus and the love that you have for all the holy ones because of the hope reserved for you in heaven. Of this you have already heard through the word of truth, the gospel, that has come to you. Just as in the whole world it is bearing fruit and growing, so also among you, from the day you heard it and came to know the grace of God in truth, as you learned it from Epaphras our beloved fellow slave, who is a trustworthy minister of Christ on your behalf and who also told us of your love in the Spirit."

If you are going to be successful in your Divine Mission, it will be necessary that you engage others to be interceding for you. And also for you to open yourself up to being an intercessor for others. This is very important, because one tactic of the Enemy is to try to isolate us in our mission. It is always important to stay connected continually be connecting with Central Command, the Church, and our Commander-in-Chief, Jesus Christ.

⚷━ⵗ You will need humility

[I]f then my people, upon whom my name has been pronounced, humble themselves and pray, and seek my face and turn from their evil ways, I will hear them from heaven and pardon their sins and heal their land. (2 Chronicles 7:14)

Pride goes before disaster, and a haughty spirit before a fall. (Proverbs 16:18)

Key Notes:
Be humble even when God does a demonstration of His power of signs and wonders, miracles and healings through you. He might even use you to raise the dead. It is good to remember that this is God doing this through us.

You must prioritize

You shall not have other gods beside me. (Exodus 20:3)

For I, the LORD, your God, am a jealous God. (Exodus 20:5b)

…but everything must be done properly and in order. (1 Corinthians 14:40)

Key Notes:
God must come first, then family, then work. Nothing shall come before God.

Consider these questions to help you to discern your Divine Mission and slowly take them into your heart and mind and ask the Holy Spirit to come into your heart as you ponder each question.

What do you love? *MUSIC WRITING CREATIVE*

What do you have passion for?

What subject gives you energy?

What people energize you? *CLERGY GUYS CHURCH*

What people exhaust you? *ADMINSTRATIVE FINE ARTS STUFF*

What do you hate and have a passion to correct?

What books are easy to read for you?

BE POLITICALLY CORRECT *YES* Are you in the general atmosphere of your interest? *PRAYER MEETING SONG WRITING*

What would you do if money was no object?

What enemies are you willing to confront?

What are you really good at? *MUSIC WRITING*

Where do you feel like you belong? *CONTEMPORARY WORSHIP SONGWRITER SHOWS*

What makes you laugh?

What do you love to talk about?

What do you love to hear about?

What focus is ever before you?

Whose pain do you want to give relief to?

Who are the people in your life that unlock your passion?

Whose voice makes you tired? *CHURCH STUFF POLITICS*

Whose joy matters to you?

Each of these questions will show you a different insight into yourself. God made you in a unique way. You have a specific way of viewing the world that no one shares. You may see a need to serve children in a hospital; someone else may be called to work with the elderly. (At the end of this section, we will walk through an example of how someone's Divine Purpose, Divine Mission, and Divine Assignments can work together.)

Another important part of accepting a call from God is accepting the authority that is already in place—beginning with God at the head, all the way to the person who will be our immediate supervisor. God is a God of order and we should have a teachable spirit and to be docile to those that exercise legitimate authority over us.

> Likewise, you younger members, be subject to the presbyters. And all of you, clothe yourselves with humility in your dealings with one another, for: "God opposes the proud but bestows favor on the humble." (1 Peter 5:5)

Your ministry might be to put the chairs away, but you would rather lead the music ministry. Just keep putting the chairs away until God gives you a new instruction. Sometimes God says only, "Wait." Usually when God is not telling us to do something, He is preparing us by teaching us a lesson or giving us information that we need.

> But when he comes, the Spirit of truth, he will guide you to all truth. (John 16:13a)

> But now, compelled by the Spirit, I am going to Jerusalem. What will happen to me there I do not know. (Acts 20:22)

> Now the one who has prepared us for this very thing is God, who has given us the Spirit as a first installment. (2 Corinthians 5:5)

He's working on us. Sometimes we need to be still so that God can shape us and then, in the fullness of time, He will show us which road to take. Waiting can be hard. But while you are waiting, you should still be praising God.

Your Divine Mission is the overall action that you are given to do while on this earth.

CHAPTER 6
DIVINE ASSIGNMENT

There are two ways to view our Divine Assignments within our Divine Mission. The first is our geography—where we are or where we are supposed to be at a given time. The second is the series of things that God asks us to do on the way to, or as part of, our Divine Mission. Our Divine Mission is general; however, a Divine Assignment is usually very specific.

First, let's discuss our Divine Assignment as our place in the world; where we are located, or should be located, for our Divine Mission. We need to be open to the prompting of the Holy Spirit about where we live. Where is God calling us to be at this moment in our lives. Some people are called to be missionaries for the Church, which can mean relocating to another country to share the Gospel. Others, however, are called to serve the Body of Christ where they were born—perhaps never moving out of their given location. Sometimes, our Divine Assignment can be to a people in a specific city or at our job location—where we work daily, or the means by which we travel to work every day. Your geography really does matter.

Next, let's examine our Divine Assignments as tasks. Divine Assignments are the things that God asks us to do on the way to our Divine Mission. Our Divine Mission is general; however, a Divine Assignment is usually very specific. All of us have a mission to get to the house of the Lord, to Heaven, and to help others to get there. Even Jesus had a mission—nothing could stop Him from going to Jerusalem; where He would suffer, die, and rise again.

When Satan was trying to stop Jesus from entering into His Passion by using Peter to think and speak in a wrong way, Jesus rebuked the Devil who was influencing Peter by saying, "Get behind me Satan."

> He turned and said to Peter, "Get behind me, Satan!
> You are an obstacle to me. You are thinking not as
> God does, but as human beings do." (Matthew
> 16:23)

It is important to realize that we have free will and can refuse a Divine Assignment. There are three types of will: our free will (we are free to choose how we will act), God's permissive will (not

God's perfect will, but He will allow it), and God's perfect will (aligning our free will with God's perfect will).

The prime example of this in Scripture is the prophet Jonah. God's perfect will for Jonah was to go to the people of Nineveh and speak to them on His behalf. Jonah chose to exercise his free will initially and went in the opposite direction.

> The word of the Lord came to Jonah, a son of Amittai: Set out for the great city of Nineveh, and preach against it; for their wickedness has come before me. But Jonah made ready to flee to Tarshish, away from the LORD. He went down to Joppa, found a ship going to Tarshish, paid the fare, and went down in it to go with them to Tarshish, away from the Lord. (Jonah 1:1-3)

Jonah had the Divine Mission to go and preach repentance to Nineveh. In order to accomplish his mission, God gave him several Divine Assignments. His placement assignment was Nineveh—that is where he was supposed to be located at that particular time. Jonah also had task assignments:

- Travel to Nineveh
- Preach against the wickedness of the city
- Help the people of Nineveh to know that they should repent

Instead of following the prompting of God and carrying out his Divine Mission and Assignments, Jonah got into a ship and ran in the opposite direction. You can do this as well. God always gives us a choice. We should be aware though, that, like Jonah, if you are not operating in your Divine Assignment you tend to make most people around you miserable and you might find yourself in the belly of a whale. Look at what happened to Jonah:

> The Lord, however, hurled a great wind upon the sea, and the storm was so great that the ship was about to break up. Then the sailors were afraid and each one cried to his god. To lighten the ship for themselves, they threw its cargo into the sea. Meanwhile, Jonah had gone down into the hold of the ship and lay there fast asleep. The captain approached him and said, "What are you doing asleep? Get up, call on your god! Perhaps this god will be mindful of us so that we will not perish." Then they said to one another, "Come let us cast lots to discover on whose account this evil has come to us." So they cast lots, and the lot fell on Jonah. (Jonah 1:4-7)

Jonah was then thrown overboard but the Lord saved him, sending a large fish to swallow him whole. Jonah spent three days and three nights in the fish's belly, until, "the Lord commanded the fish to vomit Jonah upon dry land." (Jonah 2:11) Then the Lord asked him to go to Nineveh again and this time Jonah obeyed. God continued to put Jonah back on track so that he could pick up his "list" of Divine Assignments and complete his Divine Mission.

The Book of Ruth tells of another person who received a Divine Assignment from God. Ruth was a Moabite, the daughter-in-law of Naomi, who had lost her husband and two sons. Naomi had another daughter-in-law as well—Orpah. Naomi decides that she is going to return to Bethlehem, which is her homeland. She tells her two daughters-in-law to go back to their mothers' houses, that she has nothing to offer them and they have no reason to stay with her.

Both women protest but Orpah eventually agrees and leaves. Ruth, on the other hand, decides to stay with Naomi proclaiming, "Wherever you go I will go, wherever you lodge I will lodge. Your people shall be my people and your God, my God. Where you die I will die, and there be buried. May the Lord do thus to me, and more, if even death separates me from you!" (Ruth 1:16b-17).

Ruth does this because she recognized that her Divine Assignment was to be beside her mother-in-law. It is important to be in the right place at the right time—geography matters. Poor women at this time didn't have many choices. If they wanted to eat, they could either become prostitutes or beg for food. Naomi and Ruth returned to Bethlehem together and they gathered the leftover grain from a field belonging to a man named Boaz.

Boaz was a rich young man and he sees Ruth—a young, beautiful woman who was at her right place; in her Divine Assignment. She is where she's supposed to be at that moment.

Ruth ended up married to Boaz, and they had a son named Obed. Following the genealogy found in Matthew, we find that Obed's line goes to Joseph, who was betrothed to a girl named Mary, and Mary had a child, and His name was Jesus.

All of this happened because Ruth was in her Divine Assignment (in her Field of Blessing—her correct geographical location). The Divine Assignments that we will enter into today will have eternal implications.

SEVEN (7) SIGNS THAT YOU ARE IN YOUR DIVINE ASSIGNMENT

If you are in your Divine Assignment, there is a passion in you.

When the days for his being taken up were fulfilled, he resolutely determined to journey to Jerusalem. (Luke 9:51)

There's a glory and beauty in you that comes from being a child of God and having confidence from that.

Jesse had the young man brought to them. He was ruddy, a youth with beautiful eyes, and good looking. The LORD said: There—anoint him, for this is the one! (1 Samuel 16:12)

Because you are a dreamer, you are able to inspire others.

'It will come to pass in the last days,' God says, 'that I will pour out a portion of my spirit upon all flesh. Your sons and your daughters shall prophesy, your young men shall see visions, your old men shall dream dreams. (Acts 2:17)

There is a distinct anointing on you for your Divine Assignment that is attractive to others.

But you have the anointing that comes from the holy one, and you all have knowledge. (1 John 2:20)

⊕—✶If the Lord's anointing is upon you, no one and nothing can withstand you.

What then shall we say to this? If God is for us, who can be against us? (Romans 8:31)

I command you: be strong and steadfast! Do not fear nor be dismayed, for the LORD, your God, is with you wherever you go. (Joshua 1:9)

Key Discussion:
There is one baptism, but many "fillings" of the Holy Spirit.

⊕—✶Obedience and anointing brings favor and victory.

But Samuel said: "Does the LORD delight in burnt offerings and sacrifices as much as in obedience to the LORD's command? Obedience is better than sacrifice, to listen, better than the fat of rams." (1 Samuel 15:22)

⊕—✶You smile more if you are in your Divine Assignment.

Go, eat your bread with joy and drink your wine with a merry heart, because it is now that God favors your works. (Ecclesiastes 9:7)

Moses was another individual with a Divine Assignment. He had a Divine Mission—to deliver the Israelites out of Egypt and to the Promised Land. As he was working on his Divine Mission, one of his Divine Assignments was to deal with Pharaoh, and Moses did not feel up to the task. He pleaded with God, "If you please, my Lord, I have never been eloquent, neither in the past nor now that you have spoken to your servant; but I am slow of speech and tongue." (Exodus 4:10b) Apparently, Moses had some sort of speech impediment; however, that did not stop God from calling him to exercise his Divine Assignment. Everyone, no matter what physical, mental, or emotional state, is given Divine Assignments by God, and it is our decision whether or not we accept them.

God responds, "Who gives one person speech? Who makes another mute or deaf, seeing or blind? Is it not I, the Lord?" (Exodus 4:11b) But Moses still wasn't satisfied. He didn't give up until the Lord grew angry and told him to take his brother Aaron, who was a "good speaker." (see Exodus 4:14) Sometimes, God sends others to help complete our Divine Assignments.

What can we learn from this? Even individuals we consider to be among the holiest of people can be hesitant to accept and enter into their Divine Assignments. Make no mistake, God sometimes asks us to do some things that can seem impossible or that may make us feel fearful. He might ask us to get out of our comfort zones, to go to new places, talk to new people, and do new tasks. But the second point is just as important: if God calls us to do something, He will give us the tools we need to complete the task. We can trust in Him.

Geography is important to your Divine Assignment. Your Divine Assignment can also be a specific task to further your Divine Mission.

Walking in Your Divine Mission

DEACON LARRY ONEY

CHAPTER 7
DIVINE APPOINTMENTS

Through a seemingly random act, you end up sitting next to a person on a plane, at the mall, or in a restaurant, and you strike up a conversation that changes you or offers an answer to a problem you have been experiencing in your life. Perhaps without even realizing it, you have fulfilled this role for another person during your life. These are more than coincidences. These are Divine Appointments scheduled for you by God.

Divine Appointments are meetings between you and someone else (or a group) that helps you or the other person (sometimes both sides), with an issue or problem. These Divine Appointments can be between strangers or with someone you know.

While we have spent time discerning which road to take and are busy doing God's work—fulfilling our Divine Mission and Assignments—God will give us a particular place to be and a person to meet with—a Divine Appointment. This even happened to Jesus. In the Gospel of Mark, chapter five, Jesus received a Divine Assignment to go to Jairus' house and heal his daughter. He was headed there when a woman with an issue of blood entered into His life. **This is very important: don't become so focused on one assignment that you miss an opportunity to enter into a specific appointment that God has called you to participate in with someone else.**

In Jesus' time, it was improper and socially taboo for a woman to touch a man in public; but this woman was in a desperate situation. She was a woman of great faith and she knew that if she could only touch the hem of Jesus' garment, she would be healed. She had a Divine Appointment with Jesus and because of her great faith, her affliction was healed. Jesus was busy going about His Divine Assignment (on his way to cure Jairus' daughter), which was part of His larger Divine Mission (salvation of the world); however, He took the time to recognize that, for the woman, He was supposed to meet with her in order for her to have a life-altering event—her Divine Appointment with Him.

We have to be on the look-out for when God wants us to have a Divine Appointment with those whom He has put in our path for that purpose. We also need to be on the look-out for when we are to be the one to experience a Divine Appointment with someone else. The key is to remember that sometimes the Divine

Appointment is for our benefit (like Jairus' daughter) and sometimes we are the one who will experience the Divine Appointment for someone else's benefit (to encourage, heal, or build them up).

After Jesus stopped for the woman with the issue of blood and cured her, Jesus then continued on His journey to Jairus' daughter (who by this time was dead) and He restored her to life. This is another key about Divine Appointments. Jesus stopped for the woman, but then He went back to His Divine Assignment; He did not let the Divine Appointment side-track Him. He did not forget His original assignment. We must try to have compassion for those we come into contact with; however, we must not let them distract us from our original call—even if we take time to pray with someone or have a Divine Appointment with someone else.

KEYS TO REMEMBER ABOUT DIVINE APPOINTMENTS

⚷—⚹When you are walking in your Divine Mission, you become a person who helps others—a Divine Helper.

Unable to get near Jesus because of the crowd, they opened up the roof above him. After they had broken through, they let down the mat on which the paralytic was lying. When Jesus saw their faith, he said to the paralytic, "Child, your sins are forgiven." (Mark 2:4-5)

"But a Samaritan traveler who came upon him was moved with compassion at the sight. He approached the victim, poured oil and wine over his wounds and bandaged them. Then he lifted him up on his own animal, took him to an inn and cared for him. The next day he took out two silver coins and gave them to the innkeeper with the instruction, 'Take care of him. If you spend more than what I have given you, I shall repay you on my way back.'" (Luke 10:33-35)

⚷—⚹You must know the value of all people.

Give honor to all. (1 Peter 2:17a)

But God proves his love for us in that while we were still sinners Christ died for us. (Romans 5:8)

See what love the Father has bestowed on us that we may be called the children of God. Yet so we are. (1 John 3:1a)

❧—☙You must keep a keen eye out for those whom the Lord has put close to you to teach you.

Attend to yourself and to your teaching; persevere in both tasks, for by doing so you will save both yourself and those who listen to you. (1 Timothy 4:16)

❧—☙We are ambassadors for Christ and must walk in our Divine Mission with this always in mind.

So we are ambassadors for Christ, as if God were appealing through us. (2 Corinthians 5:20a)

Another example of someone fulfilling their Divine Appointment is Mary, the mother of God. As soon as she said yes to the Archangel Gabriel, the Divine Logos—the Word of God—entered her womb. Mary, who was in a sense the new Ark of the Covenant, was hosting the presence of God. Yet, she realized that she was to have a Divine Appointment with Elizabeth. Pregnant, she traveled over sixty miles to visit her cousin Elizabeth, who was also unexpectedly with child. Elizabeth's offspring would be the great prophet, John the Baptist.

I want to share with you one more example from my own life of a woman carrying out one of her Divine Assignments within her Divine Mission. For my family, this woman was a Divine Appointment. I grew up without much materially and on one Thanksgiving Day when I was a teenager, we didn't have any food except for some greens. Then there was a knock on the door. Somebody opened the door to reveal a woman holding a bag of groceries. We didn't know why this woman had come. One of my brothers went to the door and received the bags. We couldn't believe it! The bags were full of bread, all kinds of stuffing, fresh meat, and other groceries. Clearly, she had just been to the grocery store, purchased these items, and brought them to our home. To us, she seemed like an angel of mercy bringing us these provisions on Thanksgiving Day. She gave us the groceries without a lot of fanfare and then she was gone. (To read more about how this woman who was on a Divine Assignment impacted my life, see *Amazed by God's Grace*.) As she came to my family, God's grace was coming into my life through her unforeseen act of kindness. She allowed herself to be used by Him. I realize now that this woman was on an assignment from God.

Notice that while this event was a Divine Assignment for this woman, for my family and I this was a Divine Appointment—we met with someone and experienced God's love and grace through the meeting that would change my life for the better.

God gives us Divine Appointments as well when we are called to reach out to our neighbor. Sometimes we fulfill them and do what we are supposed to do. Other times, we do it but delay it a bit; like when we are in the supermarket and run into someone we know who tells us how they are hurting. We promise to pray. We shouldn't wait to pray. We can do it right then. After all, we never know if we will be able to pray later. We need to pray in the moment that God gives us.

Sometimes we resist our Divine Appointments altogether. We complain that we don't like a particular neighbor. Maybe they never returned that item they borrowed six years ago or maybe we don't like the way they look, so we don't want to call them or go across the street to talk to them; and so, we miss our Divine Appointment.

We don't want to miss our Divine Appointments because each one is a step forward toward fulfilling our Divine Mission. One easy Divine Appointment to fulfill is to pray. Every time we pray, especially when we praise God as part of that prayer, it is a Divine Appointment. When we begin to praise, it changes the atmosphere, scatters the enemies of God, and invites the manifold blessings of God to fall down upon us. When we praise, we are creating an atmosphere that welcomes the presence of God. That prayer, that praise, will help open our hearts so that we are aware of other Divine Appointments that God is giving us. We also become aware of the unction that He gives us to complete our Assignments. Those Divine Appointments will help us in our Divine Assignments and lead us to our Divine Mission, which is exactly where God wants us to be. Because we love God and want to serve Him, it should be where we want to be as well.

To review, a Divine Appointment with someone is an appointment that God sets up that will profoundly impact or change a person's life in some way—spiritually, financially, emotionally, their thoughts or actions, or just the direction their life is moving in at that time. We can be the receivers of a Divine Appointment or the givers. We need to be open to the Holy Spirit moving in our lives and directing us daily to where we need to go and toward whom we need to interact with in a given moment.

Divine Appointments are meetings arranged by God to help you or the other person in some meaningful way toward our Divine Mission.

CHAPTER 8
DIVINE BATTLE

In this chapter, we are going to be talking about spiritual warfare—the Divine Battle. Satan comes to steal, kill, and destroy. We battle Satan's tactics with Divine strategies of the Lord of Hosts. Jesus said:

> I am the gate. Whoever enters through me will be saved, and will come in and go out and find pasture. A thief comes only to steal and slaughter and destroy; I came so that they might have life and have it more abundantly. (John 10:9-10)

But we need not be afraid, because fear is not from God. Scripture tells us that, "the one who is in you is greater than the one who is in the world." (1 John 4:4b) Jesus came to bring us life. He has conquered Satan so we can place our trust in God and have nothing to fear.

The Book of Revelation describes the battle in Heaven this way:

> Then war broke out in heaven; Michael and his angels battled against the dragon. The dragon and its angels fought back, but they did not prevail and there was no longer any place for them in heaven. The huge dragon, the ancient serpent, who is called the Devil and Satan, who deceived the whole world, was thrown down to earth, and its angels were thrown down with it. (Revelation 12:7-9)

There was a real battle, but Satan and the other fallen angels did not prevail. I love the way John says that Michael the Archangel and the angels who aligned with him fought against the huge dragon, the ancient serpent, who is called the Devil and Satan, and that Michael permanently kicked the Devil and his angels out of Heaven! The battle is not between God the Son—Jesus—and Satan. Rather, it was between Michael the Archangel and the angels and Satan and those angels who rebelled against God. Satan wanted to be God and he wanted to be praised like God.

In writing to the Church at Ephesus, St. Paul gives us more insight into this spiritual battle that all those of the Body of Christ are engaged in. He encouraged them (and us) to, "draw your strength from the Lord and from his mighty power. Put on the armor of God so that you may be able to stand firm against the tactics of the devil. For our struggle is not with flesh and blood but with the principalities, with the powers, with the world rulers of this present darkness, with the evil spirits in the heavens." (Ephesians 6:10-12).

Your battle is not against your neighbor. You may be annoyed that your neighbor does not pick up his trash can or does other things to irritate you, but that is not who your battle is with. Your battle is not with flesh and blood, but with spiritual beings, "[S]o that we might not be taken advantage of by Satan, for we are not unaware of his purposes." (2 Corinthians 2:11)

We need to always remember that we have angels on our side as well, and there are more of them on our side of the battle. This is demonstrated in the Scripture Second Kings 6:15-17:

> Early the next morning, when the servant of the man of God arose and went out, he saw the force with its horses and chariots surrounding the city. "Alas!" he said to Elisha. "What shall we do, my lord?" Elisha answered, "Do not be afraid. Our side outnumbers theirs." Then he prayed, "O LORD, open his eyes, that he may see." And the LORD opened the eyes of the servant, and he saw that the mountainside was filled with fiery chariots and horses around Elisha.

It is important to know when we are in a battle that we need to see with our spiritual eyes and not just our natural eyes. We should also recognize the reality that there are great angelic beings that are warring for us. The whole Heavenly Host is warring for us; the Angels, the Archangels, the Virtues, the Powers, the Principalities, the Dominions, the Thrones, the Cherubim, and the Seraphim. They are all on our side.

Then we have our own guardian angels, each of whom have a two-fold assignment. One is to help you and protect you. The other is to help us get to heaven. These angels are active in our world.

If we want to be in the middle of our Divine Mission—(and that is where we want to be, because we want to do the work of God)—we need to be steadfast and know that Satan is going to try to attack us. St. Paul tells us to, "put on the armor of God, that you may be able to resist on the evil day and, having done everything, to hold your ground." (Ephesians 6:13b).

When is that evil day? It is today. We need to be ready. St. Paul continues: "So stand fast with your loins girded in truth, clothed with righteousness as a breastplate, and your feet shod in readiness for the gospel of peace. In all circumstances, hold faith as a shield, to quench all [the] flaming arrows of the evil one. And take the helmet of salvation and the sword of the Spirit, which is the word of God." (Ephesians 6:14-17).

We also have another tool at our disposal to fight the enemy and it is one we can always use. That great tool is praise that we learned about in Chapter Three. Think about it. We can be feeling down, Satan is attacking us from every direction, but when we force ourselves to start singing, "Oh how I love Jesus," or whatever song God puts in your heart, or when we begin to praise God for all the blessings in our lives—our homes, our children, our spouses, our work—we will start to feel better. It changes the very air around you.

Every time we praise, it is a Divine Appointment, because when we begin to praise, we create an atmosphere that contains the presence of God. We're inviting God in to do His work in our lives. That expectation leads to a visitation, and the visitation gives birth to a manifestation. To manifest means "to show forth."

God will show His presence and His power, and that manifestation will lead to an impartation of the Spirit. That impartation will transform our lives. All of these good things will come because we chose to praise in the course of our Divine Mission.

SEVEN (7) SPIRITUAL WARFARE STRATEGIES THAT YOU MUST DEPLOY FOR YOUR DIVINE MISSION

You must not engage every enemy. You will have to be strategic in what you will ignore.

For God did not give us a spirit of cowardice but rather of power and love and self-control. (2 Timothy 1:7)

So they tried to arrest him, but no one laid a hand upon him, because his hour had not yet come. (John 7:30)

Key Discussion:
Jesus shows us the power of divinely ignoring an enemy until the right time to engage him. One of the strategies of the enemy is to try to spread us too thin. To engage us in small skirmishes instead of focusing on winning the war.

Always assess every environment that you enter into.

Beloved, do not trust every spirit but test the spirits to see whether they belong to God, because many false prophets have gone out into the world. (1 John 4:1)

Key Discussion:
This discernment must be a continual process in every aspect of our lives.

We must not walk alone; we need each other.

He summoned the Twelve and began to send them out two by two and gave them authority over unclean spirits. (Mark 6:7)

Where one alone may be overcome, two together can resist. A three-ply cord is not easily broken. (Ecclesiastes 4:12)

You will have to be strategic in how you will invest your time.

But grow in grace and in the knowledge of our Lord and savior Jesus Christ. To him be glory now and to the day of eternity. (2 Peter 3:18)

Conduct yourselves wisely toward outsiders, making the most of the opportunity. (Colossians 4:5)

You must learn the appropriate response to an adversary.

Be sober and vigilant. Your opponent the devil is prowling around like a roaring lion looking for [someone] to devour. (1 Peter 5:8)

They conquered him by the blood of the Lamb and by the word of their testimony. (Revelation 12:11a)

❖━━Every room that you enter, you bring the presence of God.

Do you not know that you are the temple of God, and that the Spirit of God dwells in you? (1 Corinthians 3:16)

"And I will ask the Father, and he will give you another Advocate to be with you always, the Spirit of truth, which the world cannot accept, because it neither sees nor knows it. But you know it, because it remains with you, and will be in you. I will not leave you orphans; I will come to you." (John 14:16-18)

❖━━The enemies of God fear you.

Do not fear: I am with you; do not be anxious: I am your God. I will strengthen you, I will help you, I will uphold you with my victorious right hand. (Isaiah 41:10)

For it is the LORD, your God, who goes with you to fight for you against your enemies and give you victory. (Deuteronomy 20:4)

"As you go, make this proclamation: 'The kingdom of heaven is at hand.'" (Matthew 10:7)

THE HOLY SPIRIT

When the disciples were afraid and in the battle for their lives in the Upper Room, God sent them the help of the Holy Spirit. "And I will ask the Father, and he will give you another Advocate to be with you always." (John 14:16) Today, the Holy Spirit is still helping us. Some of the ways in which the Holy Spirit manifests His presence in our lives are:

- The Spirit fills us and dwells in us
- The Spirit glorifies and testifies of Christ
- The Spirit bears witness in us that we are children of God
- The Spirit leads us
- The Spirit sanctifies us
- The Spirit guides us into all truth
- The Spirit empowers us
- The Spirit teaches us to pray
- The Spirit anoints us for ministry

This is just a short list of how the Holy Spirit acts on our behalf. To learn more about the Holy Spirit and what He does in our lives, please read *The Holy Spirit* Bible Study by Hope and Purpose Ministries (coming Fall 2018).

In addition to the presence and power of the Holy Spirit, there are three principle safeguards that we have that counteract the Enemy's weapons. As stated in the beginning of this chapter, Satan comes to steal, kill, and destroy. To counter those,

Christians have the Word, the Blood, and the Name: the Name of Jesus, the Blood of Christ, and the Word of God.

The Name of Jesus is a powerful safeguard, a great protection from evil. We should make a habit of pronouncing the name of Jesus out loud, over our children, in our homes, at our workplaces, in our cars, and wherever we go. When we say the name of Jesus, the enemies of God flee!

> Because of this, God greatly exalted him and bestowed on him the name that is above every name, that at the name of Jesus every knee should bend, of those in heaven and on earth and under the earth, and every tongue confess that Jesus Christ is Lord, to the glory of God the Father. (Philippians 2:9-11)

Another counter-measure to Satan's tactics is the Blood of Christ. Remember that Satan has already been defeated and that, as Christians, we have already been cleansed by the Blood of Christ, and transferred into the Kingdom of God's Son.

> He delivered us from the power of darkness and transferred us to the kingdom of his beloved Son, in whom we have redemption, the forgiveness of sins. (Colossians 1:13-14)

As Christians, we are reminded in James 4:7 to: "submit yourselves to God. Resist the devil, and he will flee from you." We, as members of the Body of Christ, cleansed and strengthened by the Blood of Christ, have only to resist the devil, and he will flee if we are submitting ourselves to God.

The last great safeguard is the Word of God. As we have shown through this book, Scripture is a powerful tool. It teaches and reminds us of the love of the Father and the protection of being under His wing. The Word of God also acts as a light to show us the path to follow: "Your word is a lamp for my feet, a light for my path." (Psalm 119:105) When we feel weak and are unsure of the path to follow, God's Word will provide a clear path and guide us.

Discernment is another gift that the Word of God is able to help us with:

> Indeed, the word of God is living and effective, sharper than any two-edged sword, penetrating even between soul and spirit, joints and marrow, and able to discern reflections and thoughts of the heart. (Hebrews 4:12)

The Word of God remains forever (see 1 Peter 1:25) and will be there for us throughout our Divine Mission while we live here on earth. It is a powerful safeguard against the Enemy. Learn to use this mighty protection as Jesus did in the Gospel of Matthew, Chapter Four. (See also Mark 1:12-13 and Luke 4:1-13.)

God allows us to be tempted by Satan; however, He also provides us with many safeguards, tools, and helps to resist the devil. One of these helps is the *"Theotokos,"* the Mother of God.

She is a mighty warrior and battles with her humility and her care and love for us. Mary, the Mother of God, who, in her humility, said "yes" to God and crushed the head of Satan. We need to ask for her protection. She says that nobody who seeks her aid or pleads for her protection will be left unaided.

MEMORARE (*ancient prayer of the Catholic Church*)

Remember, O most gracious Virgin Mary, that never was it known that anyone who fled to thy protection, implored thy help, or sought thine intercession was left unaided.

Inspired by this confidence, I fly unto thee, O Virgin of virgins, my mother; to thee do I come, before thee I stand, sinful and sorrowful. O Mother of the Word Incarnate, despise not my petitions, but in thy mercy hear and answer me. Amen.

St. John tells us that Satan was cast down to earth along with the angels who were with him. Part of the deception that Satan has worked in the world, and is working right now, is that many people believe that Satan isn't real, that he is just a figment of our imagination. In fact, some people believe that there is no such thing as evil. All we need to do is take a good look at our world to know that this isn't true. Satan seems to have free rein in almost every place.

Here's *The Good News*: the Holy Spirit is a restrainer. The Holy Spirit with His authority and His anointing is protecting the world and protecting the Church. Scripture tells us that, "the gates of the netherworld will not prevail against it." (Matthew 16:18b) If we feel like evil is starting to come against us, God will protect us. Satan does not have any power over God. God is omnipotent. Satan can't do anything with us unless God allows it. Yes, he can tempt us, but the Lord is there with us through it all helping us to resist temptation in all its many forms.

Satan likes to try to get a toe-hold in our lives by getting us to do just one little thing wrong. Then, he tries to get a foot-hold in our lives, and before you know it, there is a strong-hold in our lives that we have to work hard to break through. Therefore, we must work to resist the occasion of sin, and to repent of our sins.

There are three main ways that Satan works to tempt us: through our eyes, through our ears, and through our thoughts. King David looked at Bathsheba and saw that she was beautiful and although he had many wives, when he saw Bathsheba, he began to sin with his eyes (see 2 Samuel 11).

Sin can also enter through what we hear and listen to— challenging us about what is right and good. We should guard what we listen to every day. Our thoughts must also be guarded at all times. Jeremiah dealt with this when the prophets of his day were ignoring the word of the Lord and instead trying to delight their audiences rather than giving them the truth (see Jeremiah 4-6).

Our thoughts can also be an occasion for sin through what we think about—the Enemy tries to captivate us through impure thoughts. Keep in mind what St. Paul instructs:

> Finally, brothers, whatever is true, whatever is honorable, whatever is just, whatever is pure, whatever is lovely, whatever is gracious, if there is any excellence and if there is anything worthy of praise, think about these things. (Philippians 4:8)

In addition to calling on Mary, the mother of God, one of our other great aids in spiritual warfare is humility. Asked to list the three most important virtues, St. Bernard of Clairvaux responded: "Humility, humility, and humility." He went on to say:

> Humility is a good estate; founded thereon, the whole spiritual edifice grows into a holy temple in the Lord. Through humility, some have even possessed the gates of their enemies. For which of the virtues is so mighty to subdue the pride of demons and the tyranny of men?

True humility is not thinking less of yourself (or allowing yourself to be hurt by others); rather, true humility is thinking of yourself less—spending less time on your own agenda and focusing on God's agenda—your Divine Mission.

And so, when we are walking in our Divine Missions, meeting our Divine Appointments, and making our way through our Divine Assignments, we always need to remain humble. That's because pride goes before the fall. "Pride goes before disaster, and a haughty spirit before a fall." (Proverbs 16:18) Satan fell because of pride—he wanted to be worshipped like God. We need to acknowledge that any good that we accomplish and any good that comes our way is only through the power and grace of God.

> Then he said to me: "This is the word of the LORD to Zerubbabel: Not by might, and not by power, but by my spirit, says the LORD of hosts." (Zechariah 4:6)

We need to praise and give glory and thanks to God at all times, as Scripture teaches us: "In all circumstances give thanks, for this is the will of God for you in Christ Jesus." (1 Thess. 5:18)

We also need to know that Satan is a liar:

> You belong to your father the devil and you willingly carry out your father's desires. He was a murderer from the beginning and does not stand in truth, because there is no truth in him. When he tells a lie, he speaks in character, because he is a liar and the father of lies. (John 8:44)

He will lie to us and he uses lies as a technique to try and turn us away from God and from walking in our Divine Mission. He lies about our families. He lies about our ministries, saying, "Oh, you really don't have a ministry. You're just acting like you have a ministry. You don't have an anointing. All you have is enthusiasm." Satan will tell us all those things, but we need to ignore him. We need to stay focused on God and place our trust in Him. We need to know that we have God's anointing by virtue of our Baptism and Confirmation.

St. John goes on to tell us in the Book of Revelation, "Then I heard a loud voice in heaven say: 'Now have salvation and power come . . . For the accuser of our brothers is cast out, who accuses them before our God day and night.'" (Revelation 12:10)

Revelation continues, "They conquered him by the blood of the Lamb and by the word of their testimony; love for life did not deter them from death." (Revelation 12:11) I love that word, "conquered." They conquered him by the blood of the Lamb. Who is the Lamb? Jesus is the Lamb. He's the same Lamb that was offered during Passover. He's the same Lamb that John the Baptist saw in the Jordan River, who came to be baptized. He's the same Lamb whom John speaks about in Revelation 22 when he says, "Then the angel showed me the river of life-giving water, sparkling like crystal, flowing from the throne of God and of the Lamb." (Revelation 22:1) He's the same Lamb offered on the altar during Mass when the priest says, "Behold the Lamb of God who takes away the sins of the world." This is Jesus, the Messiah. This Lamb, Jesus of Nazareth, son of Mary, son of Joseph, who covers us with His blood and takes away our sins and the sins of the whole world!

In Hebrew, there is a saying, *"Jehovah Tsidkenu"* which means, "God is our righteousness." That is because the Lamb Jesus has shed His Blood so that when God the Father looks at our sin, He doesn't see it anymore. What He sees is the Blood of the Lamb, His Son, Jesus Christ, who was born of the Virgin, suffered, died, was buried, and on the third day rose from the grave! This is the Lord, who will come again in glory to judge the living and the dead, and His kingdom will have no end. Amen! Alleluia! That's why we can say that we overcome by the Blood of the Lamb and the word of our testimony. And what do we testify? That Christ has died, Christ has risen, and Christ will come again. For we believe that this Lamb who was slain got up from His grave and that He is coming again in glory to redeem His Church.

God gives us the Body of Christ, the Holy Sacrifice of the Mass to strengthen us. Every time we go to Mass, we have two parts to celebrate—the Liturgy of the Word and the Liturgy of the Eucharist. The Liturgy of the Word is one serving of a two-part meal that God has provided for us. It is noted that with the disciples, Jesus did many things around the sharing of a meal. When the disciples had been fishing all night and caught nothing, Jesus invited them to come ashore, and he had prepared a meal of cooked fish. And we know that before Jesus was about to face one of His greatest assignments upon the earth—a Divine Assignment—in going out of the Upper Room and across the Kidron Valley, then to the Garden of Gethsemane and ultimately to Golgotha (Calvary), He gathered the disciples around a meal—the Last Supper.

For Catholics, God gathers us every Sunday around a table, and we share a meal. The Liturgy of the Word is first presented when the Word is read. We're supposed to eat the Word—that is, take it in fully.

> I took the small scroll from the angel's hand and swallowed it. In my mouth it was like sweet honey, but when I had eaten it, my stomach turned sour. (Revelation 10:10)

This Scripture by John in the Book of Revelation, teaches us that God's Word is for everyone. The Word given to John was for all of humanity—every kingdom, every people, and for you today. John said that the Word was sweet, but at the same time, sour. He was speaking of the reality that when the Lord comes, it will be a great and terrible day—great for those of us who believe, yet terrible for those who do not believe.

The Word of God is a beautiful Word and it lifts us up. Human words have the power to build up or tear down, to avert war, to sooth a heart that has been hurt, and to give someone a hope and a purpose for their lives. It is with our human words that we publicly acknowledge and confess our belief in God. It is with human words that the priest consecrates the gifts of bread and wine and by the power of the Holy Spirit, they are turned into the Body and Blood, soul and divinity of our Lord, Jesus Christ during the Liturgy of the Eucharist.

Today, and every day, consider making a pledge to use only words that build up, and not tear down, words that will produce fruit of the Spirit, words of love and joy, peace and kindness, and thoughtfulness, and words that will offer hope and purpose to others.

Then there is the Liturgy of the Eucharist. We're supposed to eat the Eucharist, the Lamb of God. It reminds us of our Jewish brothers and sisters and the way that they escaped the Angel of Death, who passed over them while they ate the lamb and how God provided them with a way of escaping out of Egypt and slavery. They ate the roasted lamb standing as they prepared to take flight.

> This is how you are to eat it: with your loins girt, sandals on your feet and your staff in hand, you will eat it in a hurry. It is the LORD's Passover. (Exodus 12:11)

We too are eating the Lamb, to strengthen us for the journey that we have on the way up to the house of the Father. This is so that we might have strength for the trials and opposition that may come into our lives, while we are trying to exercise our Divine Mission. God gives us strength so that we may live a holy life and have the power to walk in our Divine Assignments.

That is why it is important that the Liturgy of the Word is conducted well, that there is a clear proclamation of the Gospel from the ambo and there is a clearly preached Word from the homilist. It is also important that the Mass is said with reverence and dignity at all times; this does not preclude joy.

At the Lord's Table, the offering of the elements of bread and wine, brought forth from the people of God and prayed over by the priest of God, calling down the power of God upon the elements [epiclesis] does indeed become the Eucharist, the Lamb of God, that God the Father gives to us as an acceptable sacrifice. This Jesus, who is upon the altar at this point, is not only the Lamb, but He is the altar on which we lay our sins. God, through His humility and self-giving allows man (the priest) to consecrate the elements of bread and wine so that they may become the Body and Blood of our Lord Jesus Christ.

I remember from my own journey to the Church, that one of the things that struck me and drew me to the faith was when I was on a retreat and I saw some women going to Communion with such reverence and awe. Their reverence for the Bread of Heaven, the Eucharist, touched my heart. The beauty seen in the way that they received the Lord moved me. They were receiving the

Eucharist and it was obviously a sacred moment. I barely knew what the Eucharist was, but I saw their reverence, and, at that time, a great thirst welled up in me. I had been reading John 6:53-56:

> Jesus said to them, "Amen, amen, I say to you, unless you eat the flesh of the Son of Man and drink his blood, you do not have life within you. Whoever eats my flesh and drinks my blood has eternal life, and I will raise him on the last day. For my flesh is true food, and my blood is true drink. Whoever eats my flesh and drinks my blood remains in me and I in him.

Seeing that scene of them disposing themselves to receive the Eucharist and meditating upon this Scripture caused a great thirst for the Eucharist in me. I don't know how God supernaturally did that, but it made so much sense to me then, as it does now. I often recall that I sensed a hunger, a thirst, a deep desire, and I recall when I was baptized and received first communion how powerful those moments were to me at the age of twenty-seven. Receiving the Lord in Communion is still very powerful for me every time that I am able to receive at the Lord's Table, and I look forward to those moments because they bring strength, renewal, and refreshment every time!

This is a part of what God wants to do for every member of the Body of Christ—to feed us with His own self, to encourage us, to build us up, to connect us in a fresh way to His resplendent glory, to His power, and to His majesty.

God doesn't want us to be lone wolves, because this makes us vulnerable to the Enemy. Mark 6:7 tells us Jesus, "summoned the Twelve and began to send them out two by two and gave them authority over unclean spirits." Jesus knew that, when one was weak, the other might be able to strengthen him and pull him up. God doesn't want us to walk alone. He gives us the Holy Spirit, but he also gives us those to journey with us. As we're going about doing our Divine Assignments and keeping our Divine Appointments, He wants us to be journeying with other brothers and sisters that are part of the Body of Christ that He has preordained for us to be linked with, to be in solidarity with, and in some cases to labor with during a specific season.

One way to do this is to join a Bible study or a prayer group. (For information on the Hope and Purpose Bible Study line, please visit our website at www.HopeAndPurpose.org.) These groups are directed to be short meetings and they can be a source of refreshment during the week as we prepare to head toward the Table, the Liturgy of the Word, and the Liturgy of the Eucharist. This is not a change of anything that has been handed down by our elder brothers, but this is adjusting to the realities of the speed of the modern society that we live in today, with the aim of trying to advance the Kingdom of God.

SCRIPTURES TO COMBAT FEAR WHILE WALKING IN YOUR DIVINE MISSION

📖 "The LORD is with me; I am not afraid; what can mortals do against me?" (Psalm 118:6)

📖 "They conquered him by the blood of the Lamb and by the word of their testimony; love for life did not deter them from death." (Revelation 12:11)

📖 "Though an army encamp against me, my heart does not fear; Though war be waged against me, even then do I trust." (Psalm 27:3)

📖 "Even though I walk through the valley of the shadow of death, I will fear no evil, for you are with me; your rod and your staff comfort me." (Psalm 23:4)

📖 "The LORD is my light and my salvation; whom should I fear? The LORD is my life's refuge; of whom should I be afraid?" (Psalm 27:1)

📖 "Thus we may say with confidence: 'The Lord is my helper, [and] I will not be afraid. What can anyone do to me?'" (Hebrews 13:6)

📖 "You belong to God, children, and you have conquered them, for the one who is in you is greater than the one who is in the world." (1 John 4:4)

📖 "Do not fear: I am with you; do not be anxious: I am your God. I will strengthen you, I will help you, I will uphold you with my victorious right hand." (Isaiah 41:10)

📖 "Have no anxiety at all, but in everything, by prayer and petition, with thanksgiving, make your requests known to God. Then the peace of God that surpasses all understanding will guard your hearts and minds in Christ Jesus." (Philippians 4:6-7)

📖 "I command you: be strong and steadfast! Do not fear nor be dismayed, for the LORD, your God, is with you wherever you go." (Joshua 1:9)

📖 "So humble yourselves under the mighty hand of God, that he may exalt you in due time. Cast all your worries upon him because he cares for you." (1 Peter 5:6-7)

📖 "Say to the fearful of heart: Be strong, do not fear! Here is your God, he comes with vindication; With divine recompense he comes to save you." (Isaiah 35:4)

📖 "The angel of the LORD encamps around those who fear him, and he saves them." (Psalm 34:8)

📖 "I sought the LORD, and he answered me, delivered me from all my fears." (Psalm 34:5)

📖 "He touched me with his right hand and said, 'Do not be afraid. I am the first and the last.'" (Revelation 1:17b)

📖 "For I am convinced that neither death, nor life, nor angels, nor principalities, nor present things, nor future things, nor powers, nor height, nor depth, nor any other creature will be able to separate us from the love of God in Christ Jesus our Lord." (Romans 8:38-39)

Many groups get together to prepare for Mass by reading the Scriptures ahead of time and trying to meditate on them so they can prepare their hearts to receive the Word of God more fully. This preparation for the Mass can also help us to develop a deeper understanding of the Eucharist, so that when we participate in the Liturgy of the Eucharist we can be strengthened for the week to come. I strongly recommend a supplement to the study of the weekly readings using a Catholic commentary to keep you focused and to ensure that the magisterium (the teaching authority of the Church) and its insights in regard to the Scripture are not compromised. The Bible commentary by Dr. Mary Healy on the Gospel of Mark is an excellent commentary.

We need one another. St. Paul says, "We should not stay away from our assembly, as is the custom of some, but encourage one another, and this all the more as you see the day drawing near." (Hebrews 10:25) The reason he said that is because he knew that the Enemy will try to weaken us. What happens when we gather as a community? First, there's fellowship with the Body of Christ, because the gifts that you and I have are meant for the whole Body of Christ, and those gifts are shared when the community is gathered. One has a gift of singing unto the Lord—one has the gift of encouraging—one might have the gift of healing—another has the gift of discernment. Those gifts are there to build up the Body of Christ. They're not for ourselves, but they are to be given away to the Body of Christ. We need to have relationships with people as we continue on our journey and as we enter into our Divine Mission and Divine Assignments.

We know that when we are in our Divine Mission and Divine Assignments, we certainly experience spiritual warfare. The Enemy wants to destroy our prophetic, priestly, and kingly anointing as it indicated in *Christifideles*. Every lay person is called to participate in the prophetic, priestly, and kingly mission of Jesus. We need to protect that mission, but we do not need to be afraid. We are not always going to enter into our Divine Mission and Divine Assignments easily. Those of us who are already in the midst of our Divine Mission know this to be true. We need not be afraid of spiritual warfare.

> No trial has come to you but what is human. God is faithful and will not let you be tried beyond your strength; but with the trial he will also provide a way out, so that you may be able to bear it. (1 Corinthians 10:13)

God gives us the Holy Spirit, the name of Jesus, the Blood of Christ, the Word of God, the angels, and the Eucharist to strengthen us. He gives us the Church, Mary, and the whole body of believers, the Saints and the Martyrs—the great cloud of witnesses that have gone before us. God is merciful and kind and He never forsakes His people.

**There is a Divine Battle going on,
but the Victory has already been won by Jesus.
We have Divine Assistance while
we walk in our Divine Mission.**

CHAPTER 9
DIVINE VICTORY

Throughout this book, we have explored our **Divine Hope**—Jesus Christ—and how to have a **Divine Encounter** with Christ. Next, we looked at how we go through **Divine Preparation** again and again throughout our spiritual journeys. After discovering our **Divine Purpose**, we examined the reality that we may not easily enter into our **Divine Mission**. Once our **Divine Mission** was clear, we noted that we have to have a sensitivity to **Divine Assignments** along the way—both geography and tasks.

God does not leave us to this spiritual walk alone; rather He provides us with **Divine Appointments**—both as givers and as receivers. Later, we discussed the **Divine Battle** that we are in and the **Divine Assistance** that God provides for us daily. That leads us to this chapter—**The Divine Victory**.

Jesus was declaring, when He came up from the Jordan River after His baptism by John, "The kingdom of God is at hand." (Mark 1:15b) He wasn't saying that the Kingdom of God was coming someday, He said the Kingdom of God is at hand! Jesus presented Himself after His time of Divine Preparation—the Kingdom of God was being manifest in the Person of Jesus Christ, so it was at hand.

God's Kingdom is established upon the earth, but the kingdom of this world is not God's kingdom, but a kingdom of darkness. Every believer is in the Body of Christ and is a part of the Kingdom of God. But the Enemy of God has his own associations and connections as well. We are sojourners here. Our Kingdom will be manifested fully when we are in Heaven with the Father, the Son, and the Holy Spirit.

One of the ways we can make manifest the Kingdom of God on earth is recognizing that we have a kingly, prophetic, and priestly anointing—every Christian has this. The gifts of the Holy Spirit are for the entire Body of Christ. When we go somewhere, because the DNA of God remains in us, we bring the Kingdom of God because of the presence of the Holy Spirit in us and because we are present there. We should carry that out and develop our spirituality by studying, reading, and trying to grow in humility. St. Paul lists many ways that we can grow, telling us that we should not always be looking to continue on milk, but learn how to eat meat. Hebrews 5:12-14 reads:

> Although you should be teachers by this time, you need to have someone teach you again the basic elements of the utterances of God. You need milk, [and] not solid food. Everyone who lives on milk lacks experience of the word of righteousness, for he is a child. But solid food is for the mature, for those whose faculties are trained by practice to discern good and evil.

In fact, if we are going to walk strongly in our Divine Mission, we have to learn to eat meat. We have to grasp the deeper things of God. We have to avail ourselves and open ourselves up for the Holy Spirit to continually teach us as He is a great instructor who can teach us the deeper things of the character of God. This is why Jesus said, "The Advocate, the holy Spirit that the Father will send in my name—he will teach you everything and remind you of all that [I] told you." (John 14:26)

One of the ways that we can make sure that we are successful in walking in our Divine Mission and participating in our specific Divine Assignment is to be involved with the Church. St. Paul teaches on the concept of blooming where you're planted. (see 1 Corinthians 7) Sometimes God does ask us to move, but our assignment, for the season of life that we are in, could be exactly where God has placed us at that moment. If God has placed you in a church, while you're waiting for the next instruction—for the next assignment, for the next season that God wants to move you to—bloom right where you're planted. Get involved where you are. Do all that you can do there. Humbly bring your gifts to the Body of Christ, offer to serve where you see a need, and let others see your gifts so they can encourage you and, so you also can receive the benefit of the other people there that are gifted as well. The gifts work together such that God has planted in us, in a beautiful complementary way, gifts that please the heart of God.

> How good and how pleasant it is, when brothers
> dwell together as one! (Psalms 133:1b)

I ask that you meditate (quiet yourself, quiet your thoughts, and focus on a single thought) for just five minutes. The subject of your thoughts that I want you to ponder is this: **I have a Divine Purpose. God made me for a specific purpose and plan.** Jeremiah 1:5 says, "Before I formed you in the womb I knew you, before you were born I dedicated you, a prophet to the nations I appointed you." We are not just free-floating masses of matter—God had a plan when He created us.

Our creation occurred when a Divine Person touched a human person with His breath. At that moment, divinity touched humanity, Heaven touched earth with His breath—*Ruah Kadesh* ("breath of God"). The breath of God—I use the term DNA because it's a way for humanity to understand it. God's breath in us is a powerful thing—without His breath, we have no life or being. Acts 17:28 teaches, "For 'In him we live and move and have our being.'"

God created you for a reason and one of the things we know He created you for is to be a part of His Divine Mission; to participate in His salvific mission. You and I have a part to play in gathering souls for the Kingdom, and Kingdom expansion. That is to have an effect on the temporal order of this present world and to renew it by the power of God.

KEYS TO REMEMBER ABOUT DIVINE VICTORY

⚷—∗ **If I am walking in my Divine Mission, I will be a producer of fruits of the Holy Spirit.**

> In contrast, the fruit of the Spirit is love, joy, peace, patience, kindness, generosity, faithfulness, gentleness, self-control. (Galatians 5:22-23a)

⚷—∗ **Often, right after your greatest trial will come your greatest victory.**

> "I have told you this so that you might have peace in me. In the world you will have trouble, but take courage, I have conquered the world." (John 16:33)

> For thus says the LORD of hosts: In just a little while, I will shake the heavens and the earth, the sea and the dry land. I will shake all the nations, so that the treasures of all the nations will come in. And I will fill this house with glory—says the LORD of hosts. (Haggai 2:6-7)

> At this, Jesus said to him, "Get away, Satan! It is written: 'The Lord, your God, shall you worship and him alone shall you serve.'" Then the devil left him and, behold, angels came and ministered to him. (Matthew 4:10-11)

Jesus Christ has won a great victory for you and me. The Scripture says that the wages of sin is death but we live because Jesus has walked up the hill to Calvary. He made the salvific walk even when we were still in our sins, stretched out His arms and said, *Don't count their sins against them, Father*. And He covered us with His own Body and His own Blood, and that's why Isaiah can say, "by His wounds we were healed." (Isaiah 53:5d)

One day, my dear brothers and sisters, there will be no more sorrow, pain or death. For on that day, the Holy One of Israel, the Lion of Judah will be in our midst. That will be the day that the Lord will come in glory and power and majesty.

> For if we believe that Jesus died and rose, so too will God, through Jesus, bring with him those who have fallen asleep. Indeed, we tell you this, on the word of the Lord, that we who are alive, who are left until the coming of the Lord, will surely not precede those who have fallen asleep. For the Lord himself, with a word of command, with the voice of an archangel and with the trumpet of God, will come down from heaven, and the dead in Christ will rise first. (1 Thessalonians 4:14-16)

Paul tells the Church in Thessalonica, "console one another with these words." (1 Thessalonians 4:18)

Some that are reading this might be going through trials now, but know that these trials will not last forever. One day, the Lord of glory will indeed come! When the day of the Lord comes the trees will clap their hands; justice and mercy will kiss, and goodness and kindness will dance together. And all of Jerusalem will cry out, *"baruch haba b'shem adonai"* or "Blessed is the name of the Lord." And when the Lord comes, everything will be at peace. And the Lord will say to you and me, "Come now," and He will grasp us by the hand and say, "Well done good and faithful servant. Come now and enjoy all that I've prepared for you." And the whole Church will cry out, "Amen, Hallelujah, and Glory to God!"

There is Divine Victory in the Person of Jesus Christ!

ENDNOTES

[1] "Pope Francis: anchor your heart in hope, not false security." http://www.catholicnewsagency.com/news/pope-francis-anchor-your-heart-in-hope-not-false-security/

[2] Benedict XVI. *SPE SALVI.* http://w2.vatican.va/content/benedict-xvi/en/encyclicals/documents/hf_ben-xvi_enc_20071130_spe-salvi.html (section 3)

Letter to the Reader:

Whether you read this book on your own or as part of a group, we hope that it has led to a life-changing moment for you. Please consider sharing your testimony with us as a way to encourage and build up the Body of Christ.

You may send your testimony to team@hopeandpurpose.org. Before submitting your testimony, please be sure to see our disclaimer on our website: http://hopeandpurpose.org/invite/copyright/ about the use of your testimony.

Thank you again for taking the time to read *Your Divine Mission* by Deacon Larry Oney and for considering sharing your experience with us.

Blessings,

The Hope and Purpose Ministries Team

Made in the USA
Monee, IL
29 December 2021

87515734R00075